Workshop on Question Answering for Complex Domains

Held at the 24th International Conference on Computational Linguistics (COLING 2012)

Mumbai, India
9 December 2012

Editors:

Nanda Kambhatla
Sachindra Joshi
Ganesh Ramakrishnan
Kiran Kate
Priyanka Agrawal

ISBN: 978-1-62748-360-5

Printed from e-media with permission by:

Curran Associates, Inc.
57 Morehouse Lane
Red Hook, NY 12571

proceedings.com

Some format issues inherent in the e-media version may also appear in this print version.

Printed by Curran Associates, Inc. (2013)

Association for Computational Linguistics
209 N. Eighth Street
Stroudsburg, Pennsylvania 18360

Phone: 1-570-476-8006
Fax: 1-570-476-0860

acl@aclweb.org

Additional copies of this publication are available from:

Curran Associates, Inc.
57 Morehouse Lane
Red Hook, NY 12571 USA
Phone: 845-758-0400
Fax: 845-758-2634
Email: curran@proceedings.com
Web: www.proceedings.com

Preface

Significant progress has been made in building Question Answering systems that are focussed on providing precise answers to specific questions in one shot. In many real world situations, however, the information need may be specified vaguely and some sort of interaction may be required for a complete specification of the problem. Further, the correct answer of the question may be a procedure or passage rather than a factoid. For example, someone having trouble with battery life for her smartphone may express a query as 'battery dying too soon for my XYZ phone'. The intent of the user here, obviously, is to seek a resolution to her problem. The resolution in question may be a procedure consisting of a sequence of steps. In order to recommend the correct resolution, a system may first have to engage in a dialog with the user to ascertain all the symptoms and match the correct resolution ('answer').

In this workshop, we are looking to explore such advanced QA systems that seek to resolve more general user problems in an interactive manner. We are specifically interested in the problem of rapidly bootstrapping such QA systems with limited data annotation. We invited researchers to submit papers discussing techniques for rapid annotation of Q/A pairs, information extraction, machine learning and interactive dialog for building such systems. The workshop topics include but are not limited to:

- Semi-automated data collection for building QA systems
- Crowdsourcing techniques applied to building QA systems
- Learning apriori or on the fly domain models for QA systems
- Information Extraction of problem resolutions from text
- Dialog systems for interactive question answering - clarification
- sub-dialogues, error correcting dialogues
- Building dialogue models using conversation transcripts
- System descriptions of large QA systems
- Evaluation: user centered evaluation, percent of cognitive load
- compared to search, effectiveness of interaction, quality of results

Keynote presentation
Answering Questions from Conversations

Douglas W. Oard
University of Maryland

Abstact

Perhaps unsurprisingly, the early research on question answering at the Text Retrieval Conferences (TREC) focused on answering questions from formal written text, often in the form of news stories. As is well known, that early work initially posed one-shot questions and asked for factual answers. Although our interests as a community have since grown to encompass a richer and more complex array of questions and desired answer types, formal written text is still where we most often look to find those answers. But that need not be so, and going forward it probably should not be so. In this talk I will suggest that conversations, both spoken and written, offer substantial scope for future question answering research. To make that case, I will argue from two key perspectives: (1) that some of what we seek to find can be found only in conversations, and (2) that simply retrieving parts of conversations will in many cases not be sufficient. Along the way I will illustrate my points with examples from some the work that has been done to date on meeting browsers, focused retrieval from interviews, and question answering from threaded discussion lists. I'll then look for inspiration to three emerging trends in content indexing: (1) automated characterization of social dynamics, (2) so-called "learning by reading" in which conformal semantic representations are automatically constructed from natural language, and (3) a diverse array of techniques for indexing spoken content. To wrap up the talk, I will invite us to imagine together what kinds of question answering systems we will be able to build for conversational content as these technologies mature.

Workshop chairs:
Nanda Kambhatla, Sachindra Joshi, Ganesh Ramakrishnan, Kiran Kate and Priyanka Agrawal

Organizing Committee:

Nanda Kambhatla (IBM Research - India)
Sachindra Joshi (BM Research - India)
Ganesh Ramakrishnan (IIT Bombay)
Kiran Kate (IBM Research - Singapore)
Priyanka Agrawal (IBM Research - India)

Invited Speakers:

Doug Oard (University of Maryland, College Park)
Nanda Kambhatla (IBM Research - India)

Program Committee:

Eric Brown (IBM T. J. Watson Research Center)
Jennifer Chu-Carroll (IBM IBM T. J. Watson Research Center)
Raghavendra Udupa (Microsoft Research, India)
Doug Oard (University of Maryland, College Park)
Carolyn Rose (CMU)
Indrajit Bhattacharya (IISc)
Li Haizhou (Institute for Infocomm Research, Singapore)
Cong Gao (NTU, Singapore)
Sutanu Chakraborti (IIT Madras)
Rebecca Passonneau (Columbia University)
Balaraman Ravindran (IIT Madras)
Vasudeva Varma (IIIT Hyderabad)
Ullas Nambiar (EMC India)
Shourya Roy (Xerox Research, India)
Radhika Mamidi (IIIT Hyderabad)

Diamond sponsors

Tata Consultancy Services
Linguistic Data Consortium for Indian Languages (LDC-IL)

Gold Sponsors

Microsoft Research
Beijing Baidu Netcon Science Technology Co. Ltd.

Silver sponsors

IBM, India Private Limited
Crimson Interactive Pvt. Ltd.
Yahoo
Easy Transcription & Software Pvt. Ltd.

Table of Contents

Workshop on Question Answering for Complex Domains

Program

Sunday, 9 December 2012

09:30–10:30	**Invited keynote:** *Answering Questions from Conversations* Douglas W. Oard, University of Maryland
10:30–11:00	*Simple or Complex? Classifying Questions by Answering Complexity* Yllias Chali and Sadid A. Hasan
11:00–11:30	*Question Classification and Answering from Procedural Text in English* Somnath Banerjee and Sivaji Bandyopadhyay
11:30–12:00	Tea break
12:00–12:30	*Structured and Logical Representations of Assamese Text for Question-Answering System* Shikhar Kr. Sarma and Rita Chakraborty
12:30–13:00	*Towards a thematic role based target identification model for question answering* Rivindu Perera and Udayangi Perera
13:00–13:30	*Assessment of Answers: Online Subjective Examination* Asmita Dhokrat, Hanumant Gite and C. Namrata Mahender
13:30–14:30	Lunch
14:30–15:30	**Invited talk** *Overview of Jeopardy! winning Watson system* Nanda Kambhatla, IBM Research - India
15:30–16:00	*WikiTalk: A Spoken Wikipedia-based Open-Domain Knowledge Access System* Graham Wilcock
16:00–16:30	Tea break
16:30–17:30	Open discsussion

Simple or Complex?
Classifying the Question by the Answer Complexity

Yllias Chali   Sadid A. Hasan
University of Lethbridge, Lethbridge, AB, Canada
chali@cs.uleth.ca, hasan@cs.uleth.ca

ABSTRACT
Simple questions require small snippets of text as the answers whereas *complex* questions require inferencing and synthesizing information from multiple documents to have multiple sentences as the answers. The traditional QA systems can handle simple questions easily but complex questions often need more sophisticated treatment e.g. question decomposition. Therefore, it is necessary to automatically classify an input question as simple or complex to treat them accordingly. We apply two machine learning techniques and a Latent Semantic Analysis (LSA) based method to automatically classify the questions as simple or complex.

KEYWORDS: Simple questions, complex questions, support vector machines, k-means clustering, latent semantic analysis.

1 Introduction

Automated Question Answering (QA), the ability of a machine to answer questions asked in natural language, is perhaps the most exciting technological development of the past few years (Strzalkowski and Harabagiu, 2008). QA research attempts to deal with a wide range of question types including: fact, list, definition, how, why, hypothetical, semantically-constrained, and cross-lingual questions. This paper concerns open-domain question answering where the QA system must handle questions of different types: simple or complex.

Simple questions are easier to answer (Moldovan et al., 2007) as they require small snippets of texts as the answers. For example, with a simple (i.e. factoid) question like: "What is the magnitude of the earthquake in Japan?", it can be safely assumed that the submitter of the question is looking for a number. Current QA systems have been significantly advanced in demonstrating finer abilities to answer simple factoid and list questions. On the other hand, with complex questions like: "How is Japan affected by the earthquake?", the wider focus of this question suggests that the submitter may not have a single or well-defined information need. Therefore, to answer complex type of questions we often need to go through complex procedures such as question decomposition and multi-document summarization (Chali et al., 2012; Harabagiu et al., 2006; Chali and Hasan, 2012; Chali et al., 2009). Hence, it is necessary to automatically classify an input question as simple or complex in order to answer them using the appropriate technique. Once we classify the questions as simple or complex, we can pass the simple questions to the traditional question answering systems whereas complex questions can be tackled differently in a sophisticated manner. For example, the above complex question can be decomposed into a series of simple questions such as *"How many people had died by the earthquake?"*, *"How many people became homeless?"*, and *"Which cities were mostly damaged?"*. These simple questions can then be passed to the state-of-the-art QA systems, and a single answer to the complex question can be formed by combining the individual answers to the simple questions (Harabagiu et al., 2006; Hickl et al., 2006). This motivates the significance of classifying a question as simple or complex. We experiment with two well-known machine learning methods and show that the task can be accomplished effectively using a simple feature set. We also use a LSA-based technique to automatically classify the questions as simple or complex.

2 Question Classification

Question classification is the task of assigning class labels to a given question posed in natural language. The main objective of question classification is to deal with a group of similar questions in a similar fashion, rather than focusing on each question individually. Researchers have shown that the performance of a QA system could further improve if question classification is employed (Ittycheriah et al., 2001; Hovy et al., 2001; Moldovan et al., 2003). Most approaches to question classification are based on complex natural language processing techniques which extract useful information from the question and utilize that to answer the question in an effective manner. Different rule-based and learning-based techniques have been applied over the years to tackle the question classification task (Prager et al., 1999; Silva et al., 2011; Bu et al., 2010; Zhang and Lee, 2003; Moschitti and Basili, 2006; Li and Roth, 2002).

In order to classify the questions as simple or complex we experiment with two machine learning techniques: 1) supervised and 2) unsupervised. Supervised classifiers are typically trained on data pairs, defined by feature vectors and corresponding class labels. On the other hand, unsupervised approaches rely on heuristic rules and work on unlabeled data. In this paper, we employ SVM for supervised learning whereas for the unsupervised learning experiment we use k-means clustering algorithm. We also accomplish the task using a LSA-based methodology where the main idea is to exploit a training corpus of already classified questions and then, to compare the test set questions with the semantic space of the training corpus to identify their class.

2.1 SVM

SVM is a powerful methodology for solving machine learning problems introduced by Vapnik (Cortes and Vapnik, 1995) based on the Structural Risk Minimization principle. In the field of natural language processing, SVMs are applied to text categorization and syntactic dependency structure analysis, and are reported to have achieved higher accuracy than previous approaches (Joachims, 1998). SVMs were also successfully applied to part–of–speech tagging (Giménez and Màrquez, 2003), single document summarization for both Japanese (Hirao et al., 2002a) and English documents (Hirao et al., 2002b), and multi-document summarization (Chali and Hasan, 2012; Hirao et al., 2003; Schilder and Kondadadi, 2008). This motivates us to employ SVM in our task. In the classification problem, the SVM classifier typically follows from the solution to a quadratic problem. SVM finds the separating hyperplane that has maximum margin between the two classes in case of binary classification. SVMs can also handle non-linear decision surfaces introducing kernel functions (Joachims, 1998; Kudo and Matsumoto, 2001). We consider our problem as binary classification having two classes: 1) simple questions and 2) complex questions.

In SVM, the training samples each of which belongs either to positive or negative class can be denoted by:

$$\left(x_1, y_1\right), \ldots, \left(x_u, y_u\right),\ x_j \in R^n,\ y_j \in \{+1, -1\}$$

Here, x_j is a feature vector of the j-th sample represented by an n dimensional vector; y_j is its class label. u is the number of the given training samples. SVM separates positive and negative examples by a hyperplane defined by:

$$w \cdot x + b = 0,\ w \in R^n, b \in R \tag{1}$$

Where "·" stands for the inner product. In general, a hyperplane is not unique (Cortes and Vapnik, 1995). The SVM determines the optimal hyperplane by maximizing the margin. The margin is the distance between negative examples and positive examples; the distance between $w \cdot x + b = 1$ and $w \cdot x + b = -1$. The examples on $w \cdot x + b = \pm 1$ are called the Support Vectors which represent both positive or negative examples. The hyperplane must satisfy the following constraints:

$$y_i \left(w \cdot x_j + b\right) - 1 \geq 0$$

Hence, the size of the margin is $2/||w||$. In order to maximize the margin, we assume the following objective function:

$$\begin{aligned} &Minimize_{w,b} J(w) = \frac{1}{2}||w||^2 \\ &s.t.\ y_j\left(w \cdot x_j + b\right) - 1 \geq 0 \end{aligned} \tag{2}$$

By solving a quadratic programming problem, the decision function $f(x) = sgn\left(g(x)\right)$ is derived, where

$$g(x) = \sum_{i=1}^{u} \lambda_i y_i x_i \cdot x + b \tag{3}$$

SVMs can handle non-linear decision surfaces with kernel function $K\left(x_i \cdot x\right)$. Therefore, the decision function can be rewritten as follows:

$$g(x) = \sum_{i=1}^{u} \lambda_i y_i K\left(x_i, x\right) + b \tag{4}$$

In this research, we use the linear kernel functions, which have been found to be very effective in the study of other tasks in natural language processing (Joachims, 1998; Kudo and Matsumoto, 2001).

2.2 k-means Clustering

In cluster analysis, the data or samples are divided into a number of useful subsets based on the similarity of data points. Initially, the number of subsets (clusters) or how they are distinguished from each other is not known since the training data are not labeled with the class information. k-means is a hard clustering algorithm that defines the clusters by the center of mass of their members (Manning and Schutze, 2000). It starts with a set of initial cluster centers and goes through several iterations of assigning each data object (i.e. each question in our case) to the cluster whose center is the closest. The k-means algorithm follows a simple way to cluster a given data set through a pre-specified number of clusters k. In our task, we simply assume the number of clusters, $k = 2$ since we have two clusters of questions: 1) simple and 2) complex. After all objects have been assigned, we recompute the center of each cluster as the centroid or mean ($\boldsymbol{\mu}$) of its members. We use the squared Euclidean distance as the distance function. Once we have learned the means of the clusters using the k-means algorithm, our next task is to rank the sentences according to a probability model. We have used Bayesian model in order to do so:

$$\begin{aligned} P(q_k|\boldsymbol{x}, \Theta) &= \frac{p(\boldsymbol{x}|q_k, \Theta)P(q_k|\Theta)}{p(\boldsymbol{x}|\Theta)} \\ &= \frac{p(\boldsymbol{x}|q_k, \Theta)P(q_k|\Theta)}{\sum_{k=1}^{K} p(\boldsymbol{x}|q_k, \Theta)p(q_k|\Theta)} \end{aligned} \tag{5}$$

where q_k is a cluster, $\mathbf{x}$ is a feature vector representing a sentence and Θ is the parameter set of all class models. We set the weights of the clusters as equiprobable (i.e. $P(q_k|\Theta) = 1/K$). We calculated $p(\boldsymbol{x}|q_k, \Theta)$ using the Gaussian probability distribution. The Gaussian probability density function (pdf) for the d-dimensional random variable $\boldsymbol{x}$ is given by:

$$p_{(\mu,\Sigma)}(\boldsymbol{x}) = \frac{e^{\frac{-1}{2}(x-\mu)^T\Sigma^{-1}(x-\mu)}}{\sqrt{2\pi}^d \sqrt{det(\boldsymbol{\Sigma})}} \tag{6}$$

where $\boldsymbol{\mu}$, the mean vector and $\boldsymbol{\Sigma}$, the covariance matrix are the parameters of the Gaussian distribution. We get the means ($\boldsymbol{\mu}$) from the k-means algorithm and we calculate the covariance matrix using the unbiased covariance estimation procedure:

$$\hat{\boldsymbol{\Sigma}}_j = \frac{1}{N-1}\sum_{i=1}^{N}(\boldsymbol{x}_i - \boldsymbol{\mu}_j)(\boldsymbol{x}_i - \boldsymbol{\mu}_j)^T \tag{7}$$

2.3 LSA

LSA (Landauer et al., 1998) uses a sophisticated approach to decode the inherent relationships between the contexts (typically a sentence, a paragraph or a document) and the words that they contain. The main ability of LSA is to identify the similarity between two texts even they do not have any words in common, thus providing at least a similarity score by taking synonymy and polysemy into consideration. In the first phase of LSA, a word-by-context (WCM) matrix is constructed that represents the number of times each distinct word appears in each context. The next phase is called the dimensionality reduction step. In this phase, the dimension of the WCM is shortened by applying Singular Value Decomposition (SVD) and then reducing the number of singular values in SVD. This is done in order to access the ability of LSA in determining similarity scores (other than zero) in case where two documents have nothing in common between them. To accomplish our classification task, we prepare a training corpus of two documents that contain already classified simple and complex questions. Then, the test questions are compared with the semantic space of this corpus and the question that has the highest similarity score to a document is placed under that class. For example, if a test question shows a higher similarity score with the semantic space of the document containing simple questions, it is labeled as a simple question.

3 Experiments

3.1 Data Preparation

The well-known data set[1] available for question classification is created by Li and Roth (2002). For our experiments, we have used a modified version of this data set. The original data set consists of 5,452 annotated questions for training. All these questions are labeled (i.e. annotated) as one of the six coarse-grained categories: ABBR (e.g. What does NAFTA stand

[1] http://cogcomp.cs.illinois.edu/Data/QA/QC/

for?), DESC (e.g. Why did the world enter a global depression in 1929?), ENTY (e.g. What color are tennis balls?), HUM (e.g. What is Nicholas Cage 's occupation?), LOC (e.g. What province is Edmonton located in?) and NUM (e.g. How many lawyers are there in the state of New Jersey?). An extensive manual analysis of this data set reveals the fact that DESC type questions need complex processing whereas all other types of questions are simple questions that can be answered by the QA systems easily. From the original data, we extract the 5,452 training questions[2] and then, assign new labels to them (+1 for simple questions and −1 for complex questions). The 2005, 2006 and 2007 Document Understanding Conferences (DUC[3]) focus on the task of complex question answering. They provide a list of topics along with topic descriptions (having complex questions) and a collection of relevant documents (that contains the required answers). We collect the complex questions from the topic descriptions of DUC-2006 and DUC-2007 and mix them with the previously labeled data set[4] (after assigning the label −1). Thus, we produce a labeled data set of $5,542$ questions where 4144 of them are simple questions and 1398 are complex questions.

3.2 Feature Space

For the machine learning experiments, we represent each question as a vector of feature-values. We extract the following boolean features automatically from the questions. In presence of a certain feature, we set the corresponding feature-value to 1 or assign 0, otherwise. In addition to these, we also consider the length (i.e. number of words) of a question as a useful feature. All the feature-values are normalized to [0, 1] at the end.

3.2.1 First Unigram (Which, Where, Who, What, When)

Simple questions mostly start with the unigram: *which, where, who, what or when*. We assign the value 1 if any of these five question words is present as the first unigram in the question.

3.2.2 Imperative Sentences as Questions

Some complex questions in DUC-2006 and DUC-2007 were formed as imperative sentences. These questions give instructions or express requests for some information or a particular answer (e.g. "Describe developments in the movement for the independence of Quebec from Canada."). If a question is an imperative sentence, we give it the score 1. At the same time, we also look for the question word *how* as the first unigram since a good number of complex questions begin with *how* (e.g. How do you write a book report?).

3.2.3 First Bigram (Starting with How)

The first bigram of several simple questions can be any of the following: *how many, how much, how long, how large, how big, how fast, how small* etc. We look for the presence of this type of bigrams and set the feature-value to 1, if found.

3.2.4 First Bigram (Starting with Who, What)

The bigrams: *Who is, who are, what is, what are* are often found in both simple and complex type of questions. We set the feature-value to 1 if this type of bigram is present in a question.

[2] Only questions are extracted (i.e. without their coarse-grained labels).

[3] http://duc.nist.gov/

[4] DUC complex questions are added into the dataset in order to include variety in the question space.

3.3 System Settings

For the SVM experiments, we use SVM^{light} package[5]. To allow some flexibility in separating the classes, SVM models have a cost parameter, C. We keep the value of C as default and use the linear kernel to run our experiments. For the k-means experiments, we use the k-means implementation[6] of (Pelleg and Moore, 1999). We keep the initial number of centers to 1 and use the default values of other parameters. For the LSA experiment, we use a publicly available implementation[7]. A stopword list is used to exclude unnecessary words from the WCM construction. We delete question words from the stopword list since question words are important for our task. We do not apply dimension reduction in LSA as this setting gives us the most accurate scores[8].

3.4 Evaluation and Analysis

Our data set consists of $5,542$ annotated questions. We split the data set into three equal portions to apply 3-fold cross validation for the SVM and LSA experiments. In run-1, we use the first two portions as training data and the last portion as validation (i.e. testing) data. Similarly, in run-2 and run-3, we use the first and the third subset of data for testing, respectively. On the other hand, after a number of iterations (maximum 200), the k-means algorithm converges and each question is assigned to the cluster whose center is the closest according to the Euclidean distance function. We form three different data sets for the k-means experiments. In run-1, we use $1,848$ questions for learning while in run-2 and in run-3, we use $3,695$ and $5,542$ questions, respectively. We can judge the performance of a classifier by calculating its *accuracy* on a particular test set. The accuracy can be defined as:

$$Accuracy = \frac{no.\ of\ Correctly\ Classified\ Questions}{Total\ no.\ of\ Test\ Questions}$$

In Table 1 to Table 3, we show the results for our SVM, k-means and LSA experiments. From the results we can see that the unsupervised k-means classifier clearly outperforms the supervised SVM classifier and the LSA-method for the considered task. This is due to the fact that for supervised learning and LSA experiments we need a huge number of labeled data for training. And also, the training set should be balanced having an equal distribution of the class samples. Our data set had a comparatively less number of complex questions than the simple questions. This might be the reason why SVM and LSA showed a lower accuracy than the k-means classifier. However, the average accuracy of SVM is still near 80.00% showing its good generalization ability. On the other hand, k-means classifier shows the average accuracy of 93.33% that yields the fact that it could learn from the given data set quite remarkably. This phenomenon also suggests that the k-means classifier could learn well from a skewed distribution of simple and complex questions, and this high performance is not due to overfitting on the data. Besides, the lower average accuracy of LSA suggests that the semantic understanding of the questions' content was not 100% accurate. We conduct a similar experiment with a sample dataset of 2796 questions having uniform distribution of simple and complex questions and find that SVM,

[5]http://svmlight.joachims.org/

[6]http://www.cs.cmu.edu/ dpelleg/kmeans/

[7]http://code.google.com/p/lsa-lda/

[8]We experimented with different dimensions while creating the semantic space with LSA, but, dimension reductions produced lesser accuracy in results.

k-means and LSA show an average accuracy of 83.18%, 81.64%, and 70.90%, respectively. From these results, we can see that the supervised SVM system outperforms the unsupervised k-means system when there is a uniform distribution of the question types. We can also see that the LSA system is showing a higher accuracy, which justifies the effectiveness of the approach.

Experiment	Accuracy (in %)
Run-1	79.97%
Run-2	78.94%
Run-3	79.65%
Average	79.52%

Table 1: Accuracy of SVM

Experiment	Learning Data Size	Accuracy (in %)
Run-1	1848	93.45%
Run-2	3695	93.50%
Run-3	5542	93.05%
Average	–	93.33%

Table 2: Accuracy of k-means

Experiment	Accuracy (in %)
Run-1	60.20%
Run-2	62.28%
Run-3	61.33%
Average	61.27%

Table 3: Accuracy of LSA

Conclusion

We perform the task of automatically classifying questions (that are given as input to a standard QA system) as simple or complex. This task is important because it can help a QA system decide what particular actions are needed to be taken to treat the simple or complex questions differently in an effective manner. We use two machine learning techniques: a) supervised SVM and b) unsupervised k-means algorithm, and show that the task can be accomplished effectively using a simple feature set. We also use a LSA-based technique to automatically classify the questions as simple or complex. Extensive experiments show the effectiveness of our proposed approach. In future, we plan to use more sophisticated features and then, experiment with other machine learning techniques on a larger data set.

Acknowledgments

The research reported in this paper was supported by the Natural Sciences and Engineering Research Council (NSERC) of Canada – discovery grant and the University of Lethbridge. The authors gratefully acknowledge the assistance provided by Siddharth Subramanian.

References

Bu, F., Zhu, X., Hao, Y., and Zhu, X. (2010). Function-based question classification for general qa. In *Proceedings of the 2010 Conference on Empirical Methods in Natural Language Processing*, EMNLP '10, pages 1119–1128. ACL.

Chali, Y. and Hasan, S. A. (2012). Query-focused Multi-document Summarization: Automatic Data Annotations and Supervised Learning Approaches. *Journal of Natural Language Engineering*, 18(1):109–145.

Chali, Y., Hasan, S. A., and Imam, K. (2012). Learning Good Decompositions of Complex Questions. In *Proceedings of the 17th International Conference on Applications of Natural Language Processing to Information Systems (NLDB 2012)*, pages 104–115. Springer-Verlag.

Chali, Y., Joty, S. R., and Hasan, S. A. (2009). Complex Question Answering: Unsupervised Learning Approaches and Experiments. *Journal of Artificial Intelligence Research*, 35:1–47.

Cortes, C. and Vapnik, V. N. (1995). Support Vector Networks. *Machine Learning*, 20:273–297.

Giménez, J. and Màrquez, L. (2003). Fast and accurate part-of-speech tagging: The svm approach revisited. In *RANLP*, pages 153–163.

Harabagiu, S., Lacatusu, F., and Hickl, A. (2006). Answering complex questions with random walk models. In *Proceedings of the 29th annual international ACM SIGIR conference on Research and development in information retrieval*, pages 220 – 227. ACM.

Hickl, A., Wang, P., Lehmann, J., and Harabagiu, S. (2006). Ferret: Interactive question-answering for real-world environments. In *Proceedings of the COLING/ACL on Interactive presentation sessions*, pages 25–28.

Hirao, T., Isozaki, H., Maeda, E., and Matsumoto, Y. (2002a). Extracting Important Sentences with Support Vector Machines. In *Proceedings of the 19th International Conference on Computational Linguistics*, pages 1–7, Taipei, Taiwan.

Hirao, T., Sasaki, Y., Isozaki, H., and Maeda, E. (2002b). NTT's Text Summarization System for DUC 2002. In *Proceedings of the Document Understanding Conference*, pages 104–107, Philadelphia, Pennsylvania, USA.

Hirao, T., Suzuki, J., Isozaki, H., and Maeda, E. (2003). NTT's Multiple Document Summarization System for DUC 2003. In *Proceedings of the Document Understanding Conference*, Edmonton, Canada.

Hovy, E., Gerber, L., Hermjakob, U., Lin, C. Y., and Ravichandran, D. (2001). Toward semantics-based answer pinpointing. In *Proceedings of the first international conference on Human language technology research*, pages 1–7.

Ittycheriah, A., Franz, M., Zhu, W. J., Ratnaparkhi, A., and Mammone, R. J. (2001). IBM's statistical question answering system. In *Proceedings of the 9th Text Retrieval Conference*.

Joachims, T. (1998). Text Categorization with Support Vector Machines: Learning with Many Relevant Features. In *European Conference on Machine Learning (ECML)*.

Kudo, T. and Matsumoto, Y. (2001). Chunking with Support Vector Machine. In *Proceedings of the 2nd Meeting of the North American Chapter of the Association for Computational Linguistics (NAACL 2001)*, pages 192–199, Carnegie Mellon University, Pittsburgh, PA, USA.

Landauer, T. K., Foltz, P. W., and Laham, D. (1998). An Introduction to Latent Semantic Analysis. *Discourse Processes*, (25):259–284.

Li, X. and Roth, D. (2002). Learning Question Classifiers. In *Proceedings of the 19th International Conference on Computational Linguistics*, pages 1–7, Taipei,Taiwan.

Manning, C. D. and Schutze, H. (2000). *Foundations of Statistical Natural Language Processing*. The MIT Press.

Moldovan, D., Clark, C., and Bowden, M. (2007). Lymba's PowerAnswer 4 in TREC 2007. In *TREC*.

Moldovan, D., Paşca, M., Harabagiu, S., and Surdeanu, M. (2003). Performance issues and error analysis in an open-domain question answering system. *ACM Trans. Inf. Syst.*, 21:133–154.

Moschitti, A. and Basili, R. (2006). A Tree Kernel Approach to Question and Answer Classification in Question Answering Systems. In *Proceedings of the 5th International Conference on Language Resources and Evaluation*, Genoa, Italy.

Pelleg, D. and Moore, A. (1999). Accelerating exact k-means algorithms with geometric reasoning. In *Proceedings of the fifth ACM SIGKDD international conference on Knowledge discovery and data mining*, pages 277–281. ACM.

Prager, J., Radev, D., Brown, E., and Coden, A. (1999). The Use of Predictive Annotation for Question Answering in TREC8. In *In NIST Special Publication 500-246:The Eighth Text REtrieval Conference (TREC 8*, pages 399–411. NIST.

Schilder, F. and Kondadadi, R. (2008). FastSum: Fast and Accurate Query-based Multi-document Summarization. In *Proceedings of the 46th Annual Meeting of the Association for Computational Linguistics on Human Language Technologies: Short Papers*, pages 205–208. ACL.

Silva, J., Coheur, L., Mendes, A. C., and Wichert, A. (2011). From symbolic to sub-symbolic information in question classification. *Artificial Intelligence Review*, 35:137–154.

Strzalkowski, T. and Harabagiu, S. (2008). *Advances in Open Domain Question Answering*. Springer.

Zhang, A. and Lee, W. (2003). Question Classification using Support Vector Machines. In *Proceedings of the Special Interest Group on Information Retrieval*, pages 26–32, Toronto, Canada. ACM.

Question Classification and Answering from Procedural Text in English

Somnath Banerjee Sivaji Bandyopadhyay
Department of Computer Science and Engineering
Jadavpur University, India
s.banerjee1980@gmail.com, sivaji_cse_ju@yahoo.com

ABSTRACT

Linguistic patterns reflect the regularities of Natural Language and the applicability of such linguistic patterns is acknowledged in several Natural Language Processing tasks. Many question classification systems depend on patterns that are extracted from already framed questions. In this paper, we have investigated possible question categories and question patterns for procedural text documents in English and proposed seven question classes. More than six thousands questions of different domains, e.g., cooking recipes, electronics, home and maintenance, medical etc have been collected from Yahoo answers as experimentation corpus. Annotators reached almost perfect agreement of 94.6% at kappa scale. A procedural question answering system has been developed to verify the proposed question classes. The evaluation reveals that the proposed classes are a good approach to deal with Question Answering for procedural text questions. The procedural question answering system has achieved overall 95.08%, 86.95% and 90.84 precision, recall and F-measure value respectively.

KEYWORDS: Question Answering, Question Classification, Procedural Text

1 Introduction

Automated question answering (QA) has been a hot topic of research and development since the earliest AI applications (Turing, 1950). Many international question answering evaluation tracks have taken place at conferences and workshops, such as TREC[1], CLEF[2], and NTCIR[3] to improve question-answering systems. An important component of question answering systems is question classification. The task of a question classifier is to assign one or more class labels, depending on classification strategy, to a given question written in natural language. For example, for the question "What is the capital of India?", the task of question classification is to assign label "Location" to this question. Since we predict the type of the answer, question classification is also referred as answer type prediction. Common classification strategies include semantic categorization and surface patterns identification.

Surface pattern identification methods classify questions to sets of word-based patterns. Answers are then extracted from retrieved documents using these patterns. Without the help of external knowledge, surface pattern methods suffer from limited ability to exclude answers that are in irrelevant semantic classes, especially when using smaller or heterogeneous corpora. The amount of supported classification types greatly influences the performance of QA systems.

Question classification has been studied by using different type of classifiers. Most of the successful studies on this task used support vector machines (SVM) (Zhang and Lee, 2003; Huang et al., 2008; Silva et al., 2011; Loni et al., 2011). SVMs are very successful on high dimensional data since they are more efficient especially when the feature vectors are sparse. Question classification has also been done by Maximum Entropy models (Huang et al., 2008; Blunsom et al., 2006), Sparse Network of Winnows (SNoW) (Li and Roth, 2004) and language modeling (Merkel and Klakow, 2007).

As per Wikipedia (*en.wikipedia.org*), the term *procedure* is being used in diverse domains with different meanings-

- *Organization*: A *procedure* is a document written to support a "Policy Directive".
- *Medical:* A *procedure* is a course of action intended to achieve a result in the care of persons with health problems.
- *Mathematics and Computing*: A *procedure* is a set of operations or calculations that accomplish some goal.
- *Cooking*: A *procedure* is a set of commands that show how to prepare or make something.
- *Industry and Military*: A *procedure* is a step-by-step instruction to achieve a desired result.
- *Legal:* A *procedure* is the law and rules used in the administration of justice in the court system.
- *Computer science*: A *procedure* is a part of a larger computer program that performs a specific task.

So, in general a *procedure* is a specified series of actions or operations or a set of commands which have to be executed in order to obtain a goal. Less precisely speaking, the word

[1] http://www.trec.com
[2] http://www.clef.com
[3] http://www.ntcir.com

'procedure' can indicate a sequence of activities, task, steps, decisions, calculations and processes, that when undertaken in the sequence laid down produces the described results, product or outcome. So, procedural texts consist of a sequence of instructions in order to reach a goal and range from apparently simple cooking recipes to large maintenance manuals. They also include documents as diverse as teaching texts, medical notices, social behaviour recommendations, directions for use, assembly notices, do-it-yourself notices, itinerary guides, advice texts, savoir-faire guides etc (Aouladomar and Saint-Dizier, 2005). So, the questions of procedural text are as diverse as its range of diversity. In our perspective, procedural questions will be of much growing interest to the non-technical as well as technical staff. Statistics also showed that procedural questions is the second largest set of queries formed to web search engines after factoid questions (de Rijke, 2005). This is confirmed by another detailed study carried out by (Yin, 2004).

While the first QA systems (Simmons, 1965) mainly dealt with factoid questions, a number of systems in the last decade have appeared with the aim of addressing non-factoid questions (E. M. Voorhees. 2003). Procedural questions, sometimes called 'How-questions', are questions whose induced response is typically a fragment, more or less large, of a procedure, i.e., a set of coherent instructions designed to reach a goal. Answering procedural questions thus requires being able to extract well-formed text structure unlike factoid question and analyzing a procedural text requires a dedicated discourse analysis, e.g. by means of a grammar (Delpech et al., 2008). Though less research has been conducted so far on other types of non-factoid QA, such as why-questions (Verberne et al.,2007; Pechsiri et al,2008) and procedural (how-to) questions (Yin, 2006; Delpech et al., 2008), during the last decade challenges of procedural text and argument extraction have been addressed (Fontan et al., 2008; Adam et al., 2008).

In this work, we have focused on question classification and answering from the procedural text in English and building a generic domain independent procedural question answering system.

The remainder of the paper is organized as follows: in the next section, we review the related works. Corpus preparation and system description are elaborated in third section and fourth section respectively; Corpus for procedural text and evaluation are described in fifth section and sixth section respectively; and finally seventh section describes the conclusions of our study and outlines directions of our future work.

2 Related Work

Question classification in TREC QA has been intensively studied during the past decade. Many researchers have employed machine learning methods (e.g., maximum entropy and support vector machine) by using different features, such as syntactic features (Zhang et al., 2003; Nguyen et al, 2008) and semantic features (Moschitti et al, 2007). However, these methods mainly focused on factoid questions and confined themselves to classify a question into two or a few predefined categories (e.g., "what", "how", "why", "when", "where" and so on). However, question classification in procedural text is dramatically different from factoid question classification. Therefore, traditional methods may fail to achieve the satisfactory results.

Research on procedural texts was initiated by works in psychology, cognitive ergonomics, and didactics, (Mortara et al., 1988), (Greimas, 1983), (Kosseim, 2000) to cite just a few. The issues of title identification, tagging and reconstruction via a learning mechanism in a large variety of types of procedural texts have been addressed (Adam et al., 2008). A way to retrieve the missing elements in particular predicates for incomplete title has also been proposed. The conceptual notion of instructional compounds, recognition of titles, instructions and instructional compounds has been focused by Delpech et al., 2008. A simple text grammar system that accounts for the overall text structure with respect to procedures has also been modelled and implemented. They also identified that the complexity of annotations make the task much more difficult and proposed that design domain dedicated recognizers with specific patterns might improve the low level instruction recognition results for particular domain.

The challenges of answering procedural questions from procedural text have been investigated (Saint-Dizier P, 2008) and procedural title identification and tagging, instructions and instruction arguments have also been investigated and processed. Parsing and analyzing argumentative structures in procedural texts have been addressed successfully (Fontan et al., 2008). A conceptual categorization of procedural questions based on verb categories has also been addressed for French (Aouladomar et al., 2005).Also, identification of advice and warning structures from procedural texts has been investigated (Fontan and Saint-Dizier, 2008). A quite large corpus (about 1700 texts) from several domains (basic: cooking, do it yourself, gardening, and complex: social relations, health) and a large number of web sites have been constructed for experiment and it has been found that warnings are basically organized around an 'avoid expression' combined with a proposition.

During the last decade, a number of researches have been done on addressing procedural text structure for various domains. But, those investigations were only carried out for French language and unfortunately, so far fewer researches have been carried out for classifying procedural text questions in any language.

3 Corpus Preparation

3.1 Corpus Collection

To our knowledge, similar to *procedural text* no standard corpora for English *procedural questions* are available for research. So, we had no choice to use any standard data and we had to prepare experimental data for our own. Due to broad coverage and authenticity, we have selected *Yahoo Answers*[4] for data collection. More than six thousand questions (6,230) of four different domains (cooking recipes, electronics, home and maintenance, medical) from *Yahoo Answers* have been collected and approximately six thousand questions (6,081) have been identified as valid procedural questions under human supervision. This rigorous manual work took almost 32 hours. The rejected questions were either not formed grammatically correct or posted in wrong category. Out of 6,081 identified valid questions, 4257 questions (70%) of the tagged corpus has been investigated to identify the patterns for proposed questions and rest 1824 questions (30%) corpus has been used to verify the identified patterns.

Domain	$Q_{training}$	Q_{test}
Cooking Recipe	1162	498
Electronics	1146	491
Home and Maintenance	966	414
Medical	983	421

Table1: Statistics of Procedural Questions in Corpus

[4] http://answers.yahoo.com

3.2 Pre-annotation

Collected questions have been POS tagged for the initial work of corpus preparation. Stanford Parser (Toutanova et al., 2003) has been used as the POS tagger. Then, Stanford named (Finkel et al., 2005) entity recognition (NER) tagger has also been used to identify named entities.

3.3 Annotation

Eleven patterns have been identified and used by the two human annotators. The inter-annotator agreement on question annotation has been measured by kappa statistics. The identified patterns are shown in the table below.

Rules	**Patterns**	**Category**	**Kappa-Statistics**
R1	<WH><Prerequisites><X>	PA	87.70%
R2	<WH><ITEM><VPP><X>	PA	89.60%
R3	<WH><ITEM><VPP><X><NUMBER>	PA	93.40%
R4	<WH> TO *<GOAL>*	DA	92.87%
R5	<WH><V><STEP> TO <GOAL>	DA	88.76%
R6	<WH> <Special Information> <X>	SpIA	90.90%
R7	<WH><ACTION><X>	JA	95.70%
$R7^{+}$	<WH><V><NP><X>	JA	95.70%
R8	<WH><ADV VERB><X>	AA	91.70%
R9	<WH><PREF VERB><X>	AA	94.50%
R10	<WH><WARN VERB><X>	WA	93.70%
R11	<WH><PREV VERB><X>	WA	94.60%
R12	<WH><ACTION VERB><ITEM><X>?	SIA	92.97%

Table2: Question Classification Patterns

3.3.1 Proposed Question Types Description and Identification

The objectives of question answering (QA) systems is to take a user's question of an information need expressed in natural language and seek an answer from the document collection. If a QA system is to answer questions accurately, it must accurately classify the question. The reason is intuitive: a question contains all the information to retrieve the answer. The question patterns have the ability of deciding the question type. We have proposed the following seven question classes for procedural text:

- Prerequisites Associated (PA)
- Direction Associated (DA)
- Extra or Special Information Associated (SpIA)
- Justification Associated (JA)
- Advice Associated (AA)
- Warning Associated (WA)
- Simple Instruction Associated (SIA)

***Prerequisites Associated (PA) Questions Identification*:** Every procedure needs to meet some criteria in advance or collect some ingredients to follow the instructions. These pre-criteria or ingredients are called prerequisites for a procedure. Every procedural text contains some prerequisites to follow the instructions. So, there should be a prerequisites question for a procedure. For example, in cooking recipe ingredients are the prerequisites; in Voter I-Card

Application procedure the voter should be the citizen of that nation is the prerequisite; in changing a wheel of a car puncture repair kit, e.g., needed tools are the prerequisites. So, prerequisites describe all kinds of equipments needed to realize the action and preparatory actions. Generally this type of question appears in pattern "[what|which] are the <Prerequisites> for <X>?" Where, Prerequisites= "criteria" or "ingredients" or "tools" and X= "goal or sub-goal". For example, "what are the ingredients for cooking chilly chicken?"; "What are the criterion for making Voter I-Card?"; "What are the tools for changing wheel of a car?" . So, for this type of questions the following general pattern may be considered-

(i) R1: <WH><Prerequisites><X>

(ii)R2: <WH><ITEM><VPP><X>

(iii)R3: <WH><ITEM><VPP><X><NUMBER>

For example, *"What are the ingredients for cooking chilly chicken?"*
Where, WH= "what", Prerequisites= "ingredients" ,X= "cooking chilly chicken"
"What are the criterions for making Voter I-Card?"
Where, WH= "what",Prerequisites= "criterions", X= "making Voter I-Card"
"What are the tools for changing wheel of a car?"
Where, WH= "what", Prerequisites= "tools",X= "changing wheel of a car"
"how much oil is required/needed to cook/prepare/make chilly chicken?"
Where, WH= "how much", ITEM= "oil", VPP= "is required", X= "cook chilly chicken"
"how much oil is required/needed to cook/prepare/make chilly chicken for three heads?"
Where, WH= "how much", ITEM= "oil", VPP= "is required", X= "cook chilly chicken", NUMBER= "three heads"

Direction Associated (DA) Questions Identification: Every procedure is an ordered set of instructions, Proc(X) = { $I_1,I_2,I_3 \ldots I_n$ };where X=procedure name, I_i=i^{th} instruction in the instruction set. So, user query may be on the ordered instructions associated in procedural text to reach the goal. Questions of this type appear in the pattern:

R4: <WH> TO <GOAL>

R5: <WH> <STEP> TO <GOAL>

Where, *GOAL* = "ACTION VERB" + "NOUN PHRASE"

For example, *How to prepare tea?*
Where, GOAL ="prepare tea"; ACTION VERB="prepare", NOUN PHRASE="tea"
How to assemble a computer?
What are the steps to assemble a computer?
Where, GOAL="assemble a computer",
ACTION VERB= "assemble", NOUN PHRASE="a computer"

So, the general pattern may be - <WH><GOAL> which implies: <WH><V><NP> (R4 and R5 can be generalized to R45)

Special Instruction Associated (SIA) Questions Identification: A procedural text often contains some optional information that may be very useful to the reader. This information serves a special role in the procedure. So, this information is considered as special information. For example, in cooking recipe "*preparation time*", "*cooking time*", "*servings*", "*serve with*" are the extra or special information which give the reader valuable information. In do-it-yourself domain "*difficulty*", "*time required*", "*cost*" are the extra information. Often procedural text contains one or more tips that may be helpful to the performer. For example, in cooking recipe "*serve hot with rice*" gives serving instruction to the cook. The writer of procedural text may or may not provide this sort of information. So, question may be formed to retrieve this type of information. For example, "*how long it will take to prepare tea?*" It is quite possible to find common patterns for a particular domain, but it is very difficult to form any domain independent general pattern for this type of question because special information and its questions patterns are very much domain dependent. For cooking recipe, the pattern *R6*: <WH> <Special Information> <X> may be used to classify the questions-"what is the *preparation time* for cooking fish fry?", "what is the *cooking time* for cooking fish fry?". "How long does it take to defrost a 20lb turkey?", e.g. <how long><V=defrost><X>;

Justification Associated (JA) Questions Identification: An instruction in the form: A_j because S_j, means an action instruction Aj paired with a support S_j that stresses the importance of A_j (Fontan and Saint-Dizier, 2008). For example, "Add about three cups of chilled water *to adjust the consistency.*" "Carefully plug in your mother card vertically; *otherwise you will damage the connectors.*" In these sort of instructions, the support part justifies the action part. So, this sort of instruction justifies an action to the performer. This information provides the performer the outcome or the risk factor of the action associated with the procedure. Justification associated question may be formed in the pattern-"Why to <*Action*> in <*X*>?" ;Where, ACTION="ACTION VERB" + "NOUN PHRASE", *X*="Procedure name"

For example, Why to *add three cups of child water* in cooking rice?; Why to *add child water* in cooking rice?; Why to *add water* in cooking rice?

In three example questions above, "three cups of chilled water", "add child water" and "add water" are the ACTION respectively, where "*add*" is the action verb for all examples and "*three cups of child water*", "*child water*" and "*water*" are the NOUN PHRASEes respectively. So, the general pattern can be-

R7: <WH><ACTION><X>; we can derive from R7 that $R7^{+}$: <WH><V><NP><X>.

Advice Associated (AA) Questions Identification: Procedural text also contains some advice or suggestion instructions. This instruction is identified by preference expression which may be a verb, e.g. prefer or an expression, e.g. "is advised to", "it is better", "preferable to", etc. For example, "*Cook on low heat till the rice gets heated through*", "*Cook for 4-5 minutes or till the spinach is soft*", "*choose specialized products dedicated to furniture*". These instructions should follow for better outcome of the procedure. So, a query could be: *R8:* <WH><ADV VERB><*X*>? and R9*:* <WH><PREF VERB><*X*>?

Where, ADV VERB=Advice or
PREF VERB= Preference verb e.g. "suggestion", "preferable", "recommendation";
X= "Procedure name"
For example, "*what* are the *suggestions* for *cooking chilly chicken*?"

Warning Associated (WA) Questions Identification: Procedural text often contains some action instructions that must be followed carefully to reach the goal or to avoid risk factors. Warnings are basically organized around a unique structure composed of an 'avoid expression' combined with a proposition (Fontan and Saint-Dizier, 2008). The propositions are identified by various marks- via connectors, e.g. otherwise, under the risk of, etc.; via negative expressions, e.g. in order not to, in order to avoid, etc.; via risk verbs e.g. break; via negative terms, e.g. death, disease, etc. The outcome of the procedure highly depends on this action instruction and unsuccessful action may lead to damage or harm. For example, *"Carefully plug in your mother card vertically, otherwise you will damage the connector"*.

So, performer of a procedure pay much attention about this type of instructions and forms query: "What are the warnings for <*X*>?" or "What are the instructions must follow for <*X*>?"; where *X*= "procedure name" . The pattern could be- *R10:* <WH><WARN/PREV VERB><X> and *R11:* <WH><PREV VERB><X>

Where, WARN VERB=Warning; PREV VERB= Prevention verb, e.g., "risk", "avoid", "damage" etc., *X*= "Procedure name"

Simple Instruction (SI) Associated Questions Identification: More often an instruction has no support and considered as simple instruction or instruction with empty support (Delpech and Saint-Dizier, 2008). For example, *"Add the chili powder, salt and tomatoes."*, *"Heat oil in pan, fry the onions and green chilies."*

So, queries on these action instructions are aimed to extract the timing of action. For example, in cooking recipe, the query could be *"When to add chili powder in cooking chilly chicken?*

Most of the cases, the answer may be after completion of the preceding action instruction or before completion of the following action instruction. So, the query of this type often is in the form: *R12:* <WH><ACTION VERB><ITEM><X>?

Where, ACTION VERB= Action verb, e.g. "do", "perform", "add", "start" etc., ITEM= an item e.g., ingredient, tool, criteria etc., X= "procedure name".

4 System Description

We also built a QA system to verify our proposed question classes and identified patterns. This involves storing procedures from procedural web page collected from the web. System description includes storing procedures, question classification and answer extraction.

4.1 Building Repository for Procedure

4.1.1 Title and Keyword Extraction

This process involves extraction of the title of the procedural text, prepares a list of valid keywords. Title of the recipe is determined in three phases.

First phase, extracts the title of the web file (xml, html) included in the TITLE tag. *Second phase,* extracts the text enclosed within the <Hn> tag {where n=1, 2, 3}. In the *final phase,* the extracted title texts (1st and 2nd phase) are compared. If they are matched, then one of them is taken as title, otherwise the most relevant title is taken. It has been observed from experiment that most the most relevant title is found in the first phase. Two strategies are used to determine title relevancy. In the first strategy, number of words i.e. length of the title text is used as relevancy parameter.

Title text with less than 10 words is considered as valid title. In contrast, second strategy uses stop list (e.g. click, see, buy, recommendation, advice etc) of 100 words to reject a title text as invalid title. The system uses both strategies to validate title text. The strategies are included in the present work after manual experimentation on 200 documents of the development set.

If the *title text* is "a_1 a_2 a_3 ...... a_n", then the *keyword list* will be {"a_1 a_2 a_3 ....a_n", "a_1", "a_2"..."a_n"} means that the title text with each word appears in title text. As the title text may contain preposition (e.g., the, at etc.) and some words (e.g., com, www etc.) that cannot be considered as keyword, so each keyword is considered as a valid keyword after verifying with ***stop word list***. So, the maximum size of the keyword list is n+1 if the title text contains n words and it may be less than maximum size if the title text contains invalid keywords (*stop words*). This keyword list will be processed in the next step to generate inverted index for searching.

4.1.2 Constructing Procedure Structure

The basic idea of data organization in the document is taken from (Fontan et al., 2008). Also, additional idea is introduced in data organization in order to meet the requirements of the designed system. Each identified relevant document is stored according to the structure depicted in FIG-1.Each tag term used in the structure are described below-

```
<Procedure ID= Proc_id>
<title> title of the procedure </title>
<keyword> title, each valid word in title </keyword>
<prerequisites> prerequisites list </prerequisites>
<method>
   <instructional-compound>
      <instruction> simple instruction <support> support text</support></instruction>
      <advice> advice instruction <support> support text </support></advice>
      <warning> warning instruction <support> support text</support></warning>
   </instructional-compound>
   <instructional-compound>
   .
   .
   </instructional-compound>
   .
   .
   .
   </method>
```

Fig-1: Procedure Structure

Proc ID: The system needs a unique identification number to distinguish each procedure. So, each procedure is assigned a unique integer value by the system in the first sub-module of this module.

Title: Every procedure has a name which suggests what to achieve or what to produce. For example, in recipe domain "Egg Roll", the title text describes that the step by step instruction will produce Egg roll.

Keywords: Each keyword of a procedure relates that procedure to another procedure in terms of some common matter. For example, "Chicken Roll" and "Chicken Kasa" are different preparation of item "Chicken". The "Chicken" keyword in both titles relates two procedures and describes that both item are prepared using the item "Chicken".

Prerequisites: Every procedure needs to meet some criteria in advance or needs ingredients to follow the instructions in order to reach a goal or sub-goals. These pre-criteria or ingredients are called prerequisites for a procedure. Every procedural text contains some pre-requirements to follow the instructions. So, the text attached with this tag describes the pre-criteria or ingredients for the describing procedure.

Method: Every procedure is an ordered set of instructions. So, to reach the goal those instructions must be processed in the prescribed order. The ordered instructions are described within the scope of this tag.

Instructional-Compound: Each sentence in the describing procedure is considered as an instructional-compound. So, a method is composed of instructional-compounds. An instructional-compound may contain a single or multiple instructions. The type of the instructions may be of three types- (i) Simple instruction with or without support, (ii) Advice instruction with or without support (iii) Warning instruction with or without support

Support: An instruction may be in form: Aj because Sj, which means an action instruction Aj paired with a support Sj stresses the importance of *Aj* (Fontan et al., 2008). For example, "Add about three cups of chilled water *to adjust the consistency*." "Carefully plug in your mother card vertically; *otherwise you will damage the connectors*." This sort of instructions, one part justifies the other part action. This type of instructions Sj is considered as support instruction. Support instruction may appear with simple instructions or advice or warning instructions.

Instruction: A simple instruction is stored within the instruction tag. It may or may not contain support instruction.

Advice: Often an instruction expresses an advice, suggestion or preference. For example, "Cook on low heat till the rice gets heated through", "Cook for 4-5 minutes or till the spinach is soft", "You should better let a 10 cm interval between the wall and the lattice". The advice, suggestion or preference expressions are considered as advice instruction and included within the scope of advice tag. Sometimes, an advice instruction is justified with a support part. So, an advice instruction may contain support instruction.

Warning: Procedural text often contains some action instructions that must be followed carefully to reach the goal or to avoid risk factors. For example, "Carefully plug in your mother card vertically, *otherwise you will damage the connectors*." These instructions are considered as warning instructions and included within the scope of the warning tag. In the said example instruction, the action is justified with a support instruction. So, a warning instruction may contain support instruction.

4.1.3 Instruction Categorization

Initially, all the instructions within *Instructional-Compound* are considered as simple instructions. We need to process each instruction text in order to achieve three categories described above. Three lists of cue words and phrases have been prepared manually and those are used to check each instruction. For examples,

Advice List: {*if needed, at least, if necessary, so that, allow, better... etc.*};
Warning List: {*should be, do not, must... etc.*};

Advice list and warning list have been used to separate simple instruction, advice and warning instructions. For examples,

Simple Instruction:

Advice: <advice>Cook on low heat ***till*** the rice gets heated through. *</advice>*

Warning: <warning>The paranthas ***should be*** as thin as a papad. </warning>

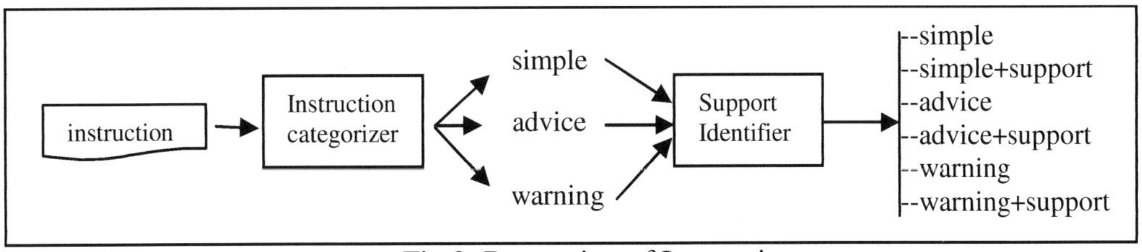

Fig 2: Processing of Instructions

Then support list has been applied to check whether the instruction includes support or not. The support portion appears in the instruction after the support list phrase. Then the input instruction is tagged properly. Support List: {*to make, to adjust, to remove... etc.*}

For example,

Instruction + Support (justification): <instruction>squeeze <support> ***to remove*** *all the oil.* </support> </instruction>

Advice + Support (justification): <advice> Add about three cups of chilled water <support> ***to adjust*** *the consistency.* </support></advice>

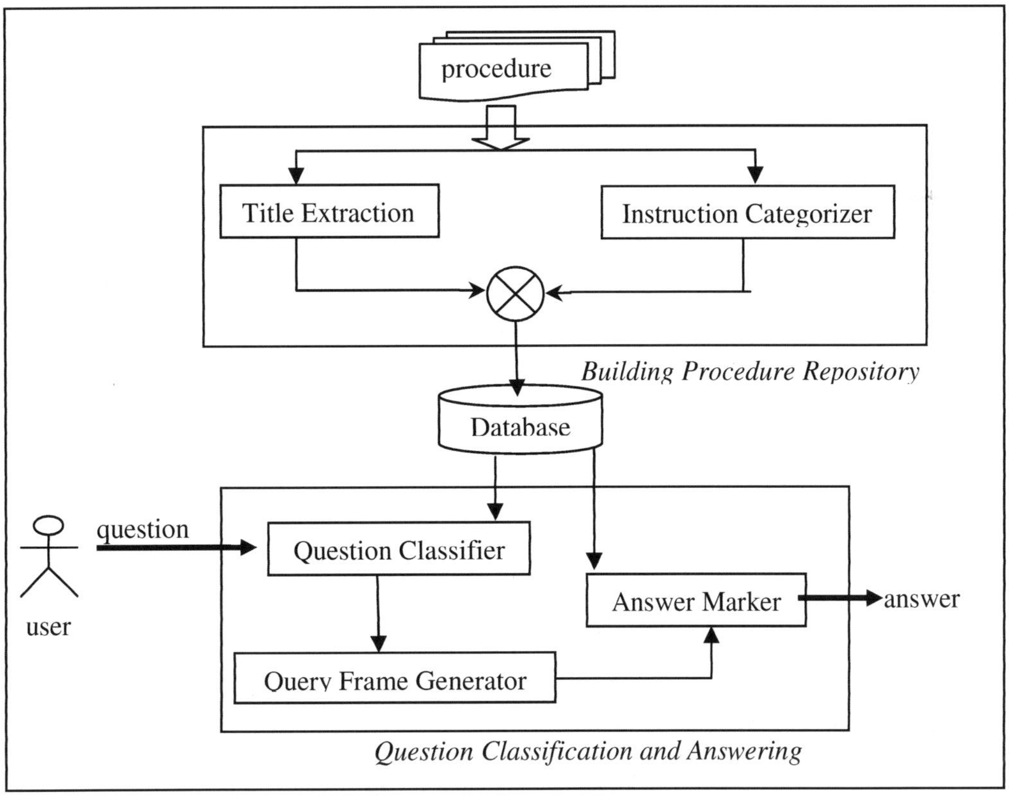

Fig 3: System Diagram

The three lists have been prepared after manually tagging 200 procedural documents. It has been observed that advice and warning cue words and phrases contains *modal verbs* (e.g., can, could, may, might, must, ought to, should, would etc.) as well as not modal verbs (e.g., had better, have to, have got to). It has been also observed that support list elements are *infinitives (to adjust, to remove etc.).*

So, if we know the syntactic structure of a language, then the model may support that language with minimal changes in the lists (Advice List, Warning List, and Support List).

If we consider the recipe domain, then prerequisites are the ingredients for the recipe. So, prerequisites list contains item with quantity. In web page they appear under ingredients header with pattern [<no>] <item> [:] <quantity> OR [<no>] <quantity> <item>, where [ ] denotes optional pattern. They can be easily extracted from the web documents.
<prerequisites> (1)5 to 5 1/2 cups flour (2)1/2 cup sugar ... </prerequisites>
<prerequisites> (1)Maida : 500 gms (2)Oil : 200 gms ... </prerequisites>

The *method tag* contains the instructions to prepare recipe. They appear in the web page under Instruction/Direction/How to make <recipe title> header. The instructions in this domain also can be identified by the instruction categorizer using the manually list of cue words and phrases. So, Advice, warning and support lists are used for recipe domain to check each sentence.

4.2 Question Classification and Answering

User forms the natural language question and submits to the system via an interface. Question Classifier module classifies the question according to the proposed question classes. This question answering system generally does not need all the information from the user input query, so a partial or shallow parsing of the input sentence is more accurate and more robust than deep or full parsing. Shallow parsing provides the structural basis for natural language questions. In the describing QA system, shallow parsing technique has been used at the syntactic level and not at the semantic level. Swallow parser generates a query parse tree (QPT) for the input question using the algorithm below-

Algorithm ParseQuestion(*NL question*)

```
Step1: node1:=find_WH( )
Step2: If ( find_Preq( ) !=null)
          node2=find_Preq( ) and go to Step3
       If (find_Action() !=null)
              node2:=find_Action()
       If ( find_Verb( ) !=null)
              node21:=find_Verb()
       If ( find_NP( ) !=null)
              node22:=find_NP()
       Else
              node2:=null
Step3: If (find_X( ) !=null)
              node3:=find_X( )
       Else
              node3:=null
Step4: Stop
```

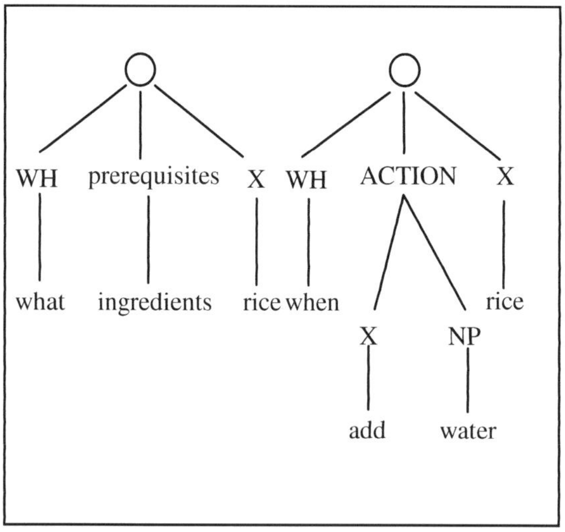

Fig-4: QPT Construction

The QPT is used to generate intermediate question pattern. This question pattern is used to classify the question according to proposed question classes. Fig-4 shows the parsing tree for the questions: *"what are the ingredients for cooking rice?"* and *"when to add water in cooking rice?"*.

Now, question pattern information is used to retrieve the documents along with the answer. For example, if question class is identified as PA question, then prerequisites tag has been marked for identified procedure.

1 Corpus for Procedural Text

We have collected 50 cooking recipes from the BBC recipe website[5], 50 electronics maintenance instructions from eHow[6]. 50 home and maintenance procedures from Home Repair[7],and 50 medical procedure descriptions from Health.Com[8]. The instructions in the home and maintenance domain are more complicated since they often involve multiple sub-procedures. For simplicity procedures with sub-procedures have not been taken. On average, each procedure contains approx 9 instructional-compounds, approx 6 simple instructions, approx 1 warning instructions and approx 2 advice instructions. Each instructional-compound is containing an average of 13 tokens (e.g., words and symbols separated by spaces).

In order to evaluate the automatic extraction system, we ask human annotators to create a gold standard against which the automatically generated content is compared. Since the system automatically identifies the instructions and classifies them into the one of the three categories (simple instruction, advice instruction and warning instruction) with or without support instruction described in the system description section, human annotators are requested to do the same by annotating the instructions using an annotation tool. For each domain, three annotators are invited to perform the task, and a subset (25%) of the corpus is used for studying Inter-Annotator-Agreement following the approach in Hripcsak and Rothschild (2005).

Domain	Instructional Compound	Simple Instruction	Advice Instruction	Warning Instruction
Cooking Recipe	510	360	102	48
Electronics	460	312	98	50
Home & Maintenance	446	281	112	53
Medical	386	230	105	51

Table 3: Procedure statistics for different domains

6 Evaluations

The evaluation set composed of 1824 questions over four domains: cooking recipes, electronics, maintenance and medical procedure. Though the test set is not very large, but it is sufficient for inductive evaluation.

We have used standard evaluation metrics precision, recall and F-measure.

---

[5] http://www.bbc.co.uk/food/recipes/
[6] http://www.ehow.com
[7] http://homerepair.about.com
[8] http://www.health.com

$$\text{Recall(R)} = \frac{\textit{number of questions classified correctly}}{\textit{total number of questions}}$$

$$\text{Precision (P)} = \frac{\textit{number of questions classified correctly}}{\text{number of questions classified by the system}}$$

$$\text{F-measure} = \frac{2PR}{P+R}\text{; where, } \beta = 1$$

Fig-5: Evaluation Metrics

Out of 1824 test questions, 1586 questions have been classified correctly of 1668 classified questions. Overall 95.08%, 86.95% and 90.84 are the precision, recall and F-measure value respectively. Table-4 and Table-5 show the statistics for cooking recipe, electronics, home and maintenance, and medical domains respectively.

Home and Maintenance								Medical						
Class	TQ	C	CC	P(%)	R(%)	F		**Class**	TQ	C	CC	P(%)	R(%)	F
PA	60	56	53	94.64	88.33	91.38		**PA**	75	71	69	97.18	92.00	94.52
DA	88	85	82	96.47	93.18	94.80		**DA**	80	73	70	95.89	87.50	91.50
SpIA	60	52	49	94.23	81.67	87.50		**SpIA**	54	49	46	93.88	85.19	89.32
JA	56	51	49	96.08	87.50	91.59		**JA**	66	61	58	95.08	87.88	91.34
AA	52	45	42	93.33	80.77	86.60		**AA**	44	40	38	95.00	86.36	90.48
WA	50	45	43	95.56	86.00	90.53		**WA**	54	49	45	91.84	83.33	87.38
SIA	48	42	39	92.86	81.25	86.67		**SIA**	48	43	40	93.02	83.33	87.91

Table 4: Home and Maintenance and Medical domains results

Cooking Recipe								Electronics						
Class	TQ	C	CC	P(%)	R(%)	F		**Class**	TQ	C	CC	P(%)	R(%)	F
PA	80	72	70	97.22	87.50	92.11		**PA**	75	72	68	94.44	90.67	92.52
DA	112	102	100	98.04	89.29	93.46		**DA**	108	100	96	96.00	88.89	92.31
SpIA	88	80	75	93.75	85.23	89.29		**SpIA**	86	80	75	93.75	87.21	90.36
JA	82	76	73	96.05	89.02	92.41		**JA**	80	74	72	97.30	90.00	93.51
AA	48	40	38	95.00	79.17	86.36		**AA**	50	42	39	92.86	78.00	84.78
WA	42	38	37	97.37	88.10	92.50		**WA**	48	46	42	91.30	87.50	89.36
SIA	46	42	39	92.86	84.78	88.64		**SIA**	44	42	39	92.86	88.64	90.70

Table 5: Cooking Recipe and Electronics domains results

(TQ: Test question, C: Correct, CC: Correctly Classified, P: Precision, R: Recall, F: F-Measure)

7 Conclusion

The simplicity of this approach makes it perfect for multilingual question answering. One can learn the question patterns for a new language using the syntactic structure of the natural language question text.

It has been observed that patterns of special or extra information associated (SpIA) question for procedural texts are highly domain dependent. So, domain specific prior knowledge is needed to recognize this type questions.

References

Aouladomar, F. (2005). A preliminary analysis of the discursive and rhetorical structure of procedural texts. In *Symposium on the Exploration and Modeling of Meaning.*

Aouladomar, F. and Saint-Dizier, P. (2005). An Exploration of the Diversity of Natural Argumentation in Instructional Texts. In *5th International Workshop on ComputationalModels of Natural Argument, IJCAI,* Edinburgh.

Aouladomar, F. and Saint-Dizier, P. (2005). Towards Answering Procedural Questions. In *Proceedings of Workshop KRAQ05, IJCAI05*, Edinburgh.

Moschitti, A., Quarteroni, S., Basili, R. and Manandhar, S. (2007). Exploiting syntactic and shallow semantic kernels for question/answer classification. In *ACL*, pages 776–783, 2007.

Adam, C., Delpech, E. and Saint-Dizier, P. (2008). Identifying and Expanding Titles in Web Texts. In *Proceedings of ACM.*

Pechsiri, C., Sroison, P. and Janviriyasopa, U. (2008). Know-why extraction from textual data. In *Proceedings of KRAQ.*

Zhang, D. and Lee, W. S. and Lee, S. (2003). Question classification using support vector machines. In *Proceedings of the 26th annual international ACM SIGIR conference on Research and development in information retrieval, SIGIR '03*, pages 26–32, New York, NY, USA,ACM.

Delpech, E. and Saint-Dizier, P. (2008). Investigating the structure of procedural texts for answering how-to questions. In *Proceedings of LREC.*

Voorhees, E. M. (2003). Overview of TREC 2003. In *Proceedings of TREC.*

Greimas, A. (1983). La Soupe au Pistou ou la Conservation d'unObjet de Valeur, In *Du sens II*, Seuil, Paris.

Hripcsak, G. and Rothschild, A. (2005). Agreement, the F-measure and reliability in information retrieval: In *Journal of the American Medical Informatics Association*, pages 296-298.

Finkel, J. R., Grenager, T and Manning, C. (2005). Incorporating Non-local Information into Information Extraction Systems by Gibbs Sampling. In *Proceedings of the 43nd Annual Meeting of the Association for Computational Linguistics (ACL 2005)*, pages 363-370.

Toutanova, K., Klein, D., Manning, C. and Singer, Y. (2003). Feature-Rich Part-of-Speech Tagging with a Cyclic Dependency Network. In Proceedings of HLT-NAACL 2003, pages 252-259.

Kosseim, L. and Lapalme, G. (2000). Choosing Rhetorical Structuresto Plan InstructionalTexts, Computational Intelligence, Blackwell, Boston.

Fontan, L. and Saint-Dizier, P. (2008). Creating and Querying a Domain dependent Know-How Knowledge Base of Advices and Warnings. In *Proceedings of KRAQ.*

Yin, L. (2006). A two-stage approach to retrieving answers for how-to questions. In *Proceedings of EACL (Student Session).*

Fontan, L. and Saint-Dizier, P. (2008). Analyzing Argumentative Structures in *Procedural Texts. GoTAL 2008*, pages 366-370

Fontan, L. and Saint-Dizier, P. (2008). Constructing a know-how repository of advices and warnings from procedural texts. ACM Symposium on Document Engineering 2008, pages 249-252

Cai, L., Zhou, G., Liu, L. and Zhao, J. () Large-Scale Question Classification in cQA by Leveraging Wikipedia Semantic Knowledge.

Mortara Garavelli, B., Tipologia dei Testi, In (G. Hodus et al., 1988: lexicon der romanistischen Linguistik, vol. IV, Tubingen, Niemeyer).

Simmons, R. F. (1965). Answering English questions by computer: a survey. Comm. ACM, 8(1):53–70.

S. Verberne, L. Boves, N. Oostdijk, and P. Coppen. 2007. Evaluating discourse-based answer extraction for why-question answering. In *Proceedings of SIGIR*, pages 735–737.

Saint-Dizier, P. (2008). Some Challenges of Advanced Question-Answering: an Experiment with How-to Questions. In *Proceedings of PACLIC 2008*, pages 65-73

Nguyen, T., Nguyen, L. and Shimazu, A. (2008). Using semi-supervised learning for question classification. *Journal Natural Language Processing*, 15(1):3–21.

Zhang, Z., Uren, V., Ciravegna, F. (2010). Position paper: A comprehensive solution to procedural knowledge acquisition using information extraction. In *Proceedings of KDIR2010, Valencia.*

Li, X. and Roth, D. (2004). Learning question classifiers: The role of semantic information. In *Proceedings of International Conference on Computational Linguistics (COLING)*, pages 556–562.

Huang, Z., Thint, M. and Qin. Z. (2008). Question classification using head words and their hypernyms. In *Proceedings of EMNLP*, pages 927–936.

Silva, J., Coheur, L., Mendes, A. and Wichert, A. (2011). From symbolic to sub-symbolic information in question classification. Artifcial Intelligence Review, 35(2):137–154.

Merkel, A. and Klakow, D. (2007). Improved methods of language model based question classification. In *Proceedings of Interspeech Conference.*

Blunsom, P., Kocik, K. and Curran, J. R. (2006). Question classification with log-linear models. In *Proceedings of SIGIR '06*, pages 615–616, NY, USA, ACM.

De Rijke, M. (2005). Question Answering: What's Next?, In *Sixth International Workshop on Computational Semantics*, Tilburg.

Yin, L. (2004). Topic Analysis and Answering Procedural Questions, Information Technology Research Institute Technical Report Series, ITRI-04-14, University of Brighton, UK.

Loni, B., Tulder,G., Wiggers, P., Loog, M. and Tax, D. (2011).Question classification with weighted combination of lexical, syntactical and semantic features. In *Proceedings of the 15th international conference of Text, Dialog and Speech.*

Structured and Logical Representations of Assamese Text for Question-Answering System

Rita CHAKRABORTY Shikhar Kr. SARMA
DEPARTMENT OF INFORMATION TECHNOLOGY, GAUHATI UNIVERSITY
Guwahati, Assam, India 781014
ritachk@rediffmail.com, sks001@gmail.com

ABSTRACT

Written documents contain information in a language specific syntax form. Computational processing of such information demands representation in a structured form suitable for handling, processing, and analyzing. Such structured representation of documents enables extraction of knowledge through computational means. Once the textual data are represented in structured form, logical representation also becomes easier. This paper discusses our work on analyzing texts in Assamese language and processing those texts in terms of converting into structured and logical representations. Our emphasis is on the Structured Representation of texts and current study focuses on providing the architecture and processing workflow of the system to output structured form of Assamese text. It also includes system design discussions on how these representations of texts in Assamese language will contribute towards building a Question-Answering system.

KEYWORDS: Structured Representation, Logical Representation, Question- Answering System

1. Introduction:

Written documents such as text documents, web pages and books contain information in a language specific syntactic form, not suitable for automatic processing through computers. Therefore, this textual information must be represented in such a manner so that analyzing and processing of these texts becomes easier [5][6]. This representation also makes automatic knowledge extraction possible. Assamese is a new language for which NLP research works have recently started analyzing and building various automated computational models. Many research works are going on for other naturally occurring languages like English, Bodo etc. Various automated tools and techniques have also been developed for these languages. The proposed research work is a new domain of research in Assamese language for getting an insight into how sentences in Assamese can be analyzed, parsed and interpreted. The structured text representation shows the relationship among the constituents of a sentence. It will provide the basis for doing higher level projects such as building Question-answering systems [1]. The information gained from this kind of representation will also pave the way for further research works related to cross-lingual information system, automatic text extraction, mining information etc [3]. This research work is expected to give syntactic and semantic characteristics of Assamese language in the perspective of computational linguistics [1][5]. We are also expecting to get a POS tagged Assamese corpus as well as computational modules for building structured and logical representations of Assamese text corpus.

Development of regional languages has been a great concern now a days. This is due to the fact that these languages are getting more demands for putting them as a medium of communication of the digital world. Researchers and government agencies have started their effort to design and develop different technologies for putting those regional languages into the digital world. Research and development of various language technologies have also started for Assamese language, which is recognized as a scheduled language of Indian constitution. Technologies like UNICODE compliant fonts and keyboards, automated spell checker have already been developed for this language [9]. Research works are also going on for developing various technologies for Assamese language as part of the efforts on technology development of Indian languages.

Assamese is a new language to digital revolution. This language is also used as a medium of communication within the states of North-East India, especially in Arunachal Pradesh and Nagaland. A huge population of India speaks Assamese in different parts of the nation who originally belong to Assam. Assamese speaking people can also be found in some nations like, Bhutan and Bangladesh. Tentatively, about 14 million people speak Assamese in the state of Assam and its neighbouring states and about 14.3 million Assamese speaking people can be found in all over India [9].

The origin of Assamese language can be derived from its relation with Indo-Aryan group of languages and a little bit with Sino-Tibetan group of languages. Apart from Assamese, languages like Bangla, Oriya, Hindi etc. also fall into the category of Indo-Aryan group[9]. These languages have similarity with Assamese language. However, differences may also exist among these languages; still, the technologies developed for Assamese are expected to be able to provide an insight into the development of similar kind of technologies for these languages. In this paper, we are focusing on the representations of Assamese text in terms of the structured and logical formalisms. The technologies built in this regard will hopefully be able to represent knowledge in structured and logical forms for other Indo-Aryan languages. This will happen due to the fact that these languages have similarity with Assamese language. Therefore, we expect to design and develop an automated model which will also be used for developing technologies for other similar languages.

In order to analyze a corpus based text in terms of computational linguistics, it must pass through different phases like- morphological, syntactical, semantics, pragmatic etc. The morphological analysis analyzes individual word and non-word tokens such as punctuation markers. These non-word special markers must be separated in this phase. In the syntax analysis part, the tokens generated from the morphological analysis are transformed into structures showing the relationship among the tokens [1][4]. This relationship must follow the grammatical rules of the language. If a combination does not follow any rule, that sequence must be rejected. The structures created by the syntactic analyzer are assigned meanings at the semantic level. The ambiguity of sentences must be resolved in this phase [1][4][3]. We are basically concentrating on syntactic level analysis and partially on semantics. The extracted knowledge using these two representations provides information in terms of grammatical structures of the language. They also provide the scope of doing analysis in semantic levels so that the meaning of the sentences can be interpreted. This paper is organized in the following way- section 2 gives an idea of related topics which outlines the idea of structured and logical representations. Section 3 describes the overall planning of the project work. Section 4 provides an outline of analysis of sentences written in Assamese. Section 5 describes the proposed model for question-answering system which also outlines an idea of Assamese question pattern and section 6 is the proposed conclusion.

2. Related topics:

2.1 Structured Text:

The context of the input text must be represented in structured text format. Structured text describes the individual objects occurring in the sentences. It attempts to capture the knowledge contained in the text essential for doing various kinds of operations. Things that are not mentioned explicitly in the given text such as references to pronouns are made explicit here. As a whole, it can be said that the context of the sentences are represented using structured text [1]. To show this, Let us consider the following English sentence-

I got the red ball that I wanted.

This sentence can be represented in structured form in the following manner-

Event-1

Instance -	Get
Tense-	Past
Agent-	I
Object-	Thing

Thing

Instance-	Ball
Color-	Red

Event-2

Instance -	want
Tense-	Past

One of the key ideas of such kind of representation is to find out the meanings of the objects with reference to their connections to other objects. Such kind of representation can also be termed as slot-and-filler structure [1]. The information gained from such kind of structure represents knowledge in terms of syntactic level. It operates as a mechanism to see whether these structures conform to the rules or syntax of Assamese language.

2.2 Logical Representation:

The structured information forms the basic building block for knowledge acquisition formalism. The information acquired in structured text representation can be used to represent knowledge in logical formalism also. Logical representation can also be implemented to acquire new knowledge from old. It guarantees that a new statement can be proved to be true because the statement follows from some already proved statements [1]. Such kind of representation can be gained through First Order Predicate Calculus (FOPC) [2]. Basically the facts and rules in logical representation can be expressed in FOPC using PROLOG. The well formed formulas representing the facts and rules should be written in Clause form only. The clausal notations can be implemented in question answering systems also. Such representation can be used to answer not only yes-no questions but also fill-in-the blank questions [1]. To show this, let us consider a sentence in English – "Rina eats mango" can be represented in PROLOG as –

eat (Rina,mango).

Now, if we have a query like –

?eat (Rina,X) gives the answer **X=mango**.

The proof procedure of PROLOG follows Resolution principle where the proof is generated through backward chaining process [1][2]. Actually, the process of deriving answers to questions using logic is based on Matching technique. Matching takes two terms as input and checks to see whether they match. If they match, the process produces a success signal. Using matching process, variables can also be bound to values if necessary [2]. For e.g. the terms date(1, may, 2005) and date(D,M,Y) match. The results of this matching process is –

D=1
M=may
Y=2005

Both structured text and logical representations for Assamese language have been discussed later in this paper.

3. Proposed System:

The proposed research work is just the preprocessing phase of doing NLP research in Assamese language. We have planned to divide the whole project work into two primary modules- The Preprocessor module and the Structured Text Generator module. These two modules are again subdivided into some sub modules. The following diagram is a structural representation of the proposed system-

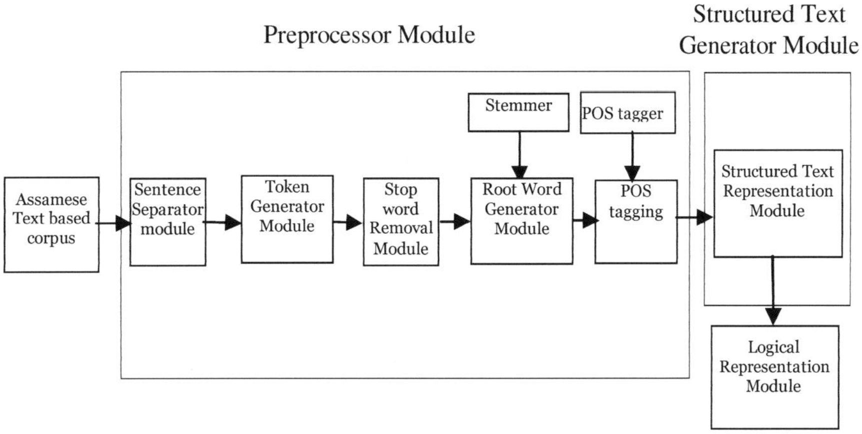

FIGURE: Structural / Diagrammatic representation of the proposed system

As shown in the diagram, an Assamese text based corpus will be taken as the input to the system. The Preprocessor module begins with the *Sentence Separator* module which separates the sentences basic to the text corpus. After that the *Token Generator* module begins which extracts individual tokens from the sentences. Next step is to remove the stop words such as the punctuation markers or conjunctives from the tokens generated so far using the *Stop Word Removal* module. At this stage, we get the tokens which are actually taking part in that particular context. Then we pass these tokens through an automated stemmer which generates the root morphemes behind every token. This is done by the *Root Word Generator* module [7]. After this, the root morphemes are annotated in terms of Parts-of-Speech (POS) tagging. Using a POS tagger, each morpheme will be tagged and these annotated morphemes will be used in the later processing of the text. These whole set of operations may be regarded as the morphological analysis in terms of computational linguistics.

Next module is the Structured Text Generator module which generates structured text from the outputs of the Preprocessor module. The annotated lexicons provide the information about subject(s), verb(s), instance(s) and object(s) in the sentences. Structured text representation will be generated based on this information. This same information can be used in generating logical representation also.

Automated validators may be required for testing these representations in terms of linguistics.

4. Analysis of Sentences Written in Assamese:

Sentences in Assamese are the well-organized sequence of parts-of-speech and inflections. Therefore, the syntax of a sentence can be termed as the rule-based implementation of inflections to the parts-of-speech of the sentence. The structure of sentences can also be termed as the structure of the language [8].

Sentences in Assamese basically follow the Subject+Object+Verb form. Actually this is the structure of a simple sentence. For e.g.

মই কিতাপ পঢ়োঁ (I read book)

Sentences may be compound or complex also. Verbs play an important role in such sentences because they help in achieving the idea about the meaning of the sentences. They have direct relationship with all the cases except case 6, that is, genitive case. The association between subject and verb make an Assamese sentence complete. Verb along with all cases except the subjective case occur in predicate part of an Assamese sentence [8]. The inflections should be incorporated into the words in a proper manner so that the actual interpretation of the sentences can be gained.

In order to analyze sentences written in Assamese, one must possess the knowledge of parts-of-speech of this language. In this section, we are producing a sentence level analysis in Assamese which has relevance with our work model.

Let us consider the same sentence- ৰীণাই আম খাই ভাল পায়

The dataflow model for parsing this sentence is as follows-

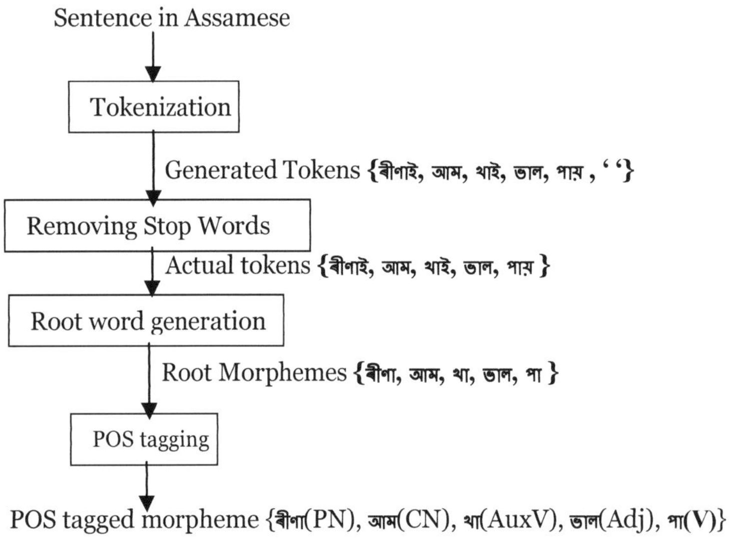

The outputs of POS tagging phase are the tagged morphemes of the root words [7].

The tagged morphemes of the assumed sentence are as follows-

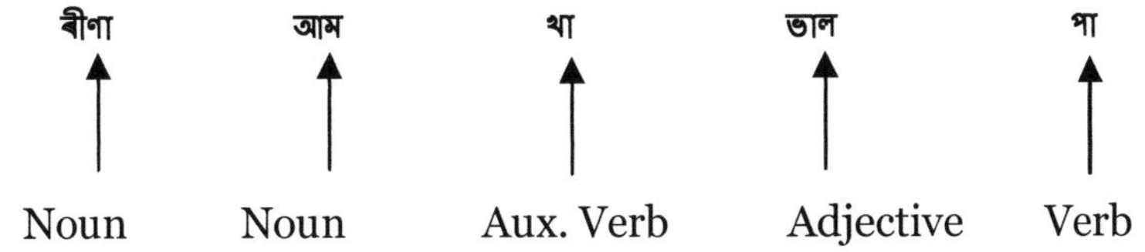

The POS tagged morphemes are passed through the syntax analysis phase where a graphical representation or a parse tree will be constructed on these morphemes. The hierarchical structure must obey the grammatical rule of the language. The output of the syntax analysis phase i.e. the parse tree for the particular sentence is as follows-

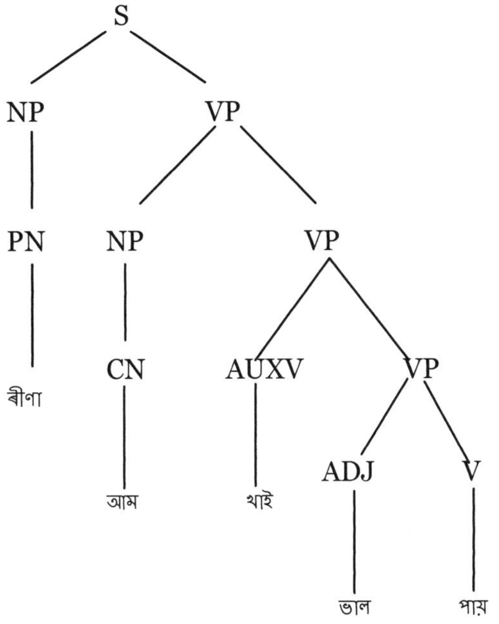

FIGURE : Parse tree for the Assamese sentence "ৰীণাই আম খাই ভাল পায়"

In this way, the sentences in Assamese will be analyzed and parsed to examine whether they follow the correct syntactic structure of the language. Any sentence structure which does not follow any syntax of the language should never be accepted.

5. Model for Question-Answering System:

5.1 Assamese Question Pattern:

Interrogative sentence or question pattern is one of the types of sentences in Assamese language. There are two factors playing important role in Assamese question patterns- parts-of-speech and rhythm in which the question is being asked. The rhythm of the question defines the kind and manner of the response being sought [8]. Some questions may be asked using do-verb in different forms. An example of a simple interrogative sentence using do-verb in present tense, second person singular number is given below-

তুমি সদায় পঢ়া নে? (Do you read always?)

Questions may be formed using কি (What), কিয় (Why), ক'ত (Where), কেতিয়া (When), কাৰ (Whose), কেনেকৈ (How), কিমান (How Much) etc. Examples of simple question pattern of such kind may be-

তোমাৰ নাম কি ? (What is your name?)

তেওঁ ক'ত থাকে ? (Where does he live?)

Questions patterns may be complex also. These types of interrogative sentences may be split up into more than one simple questions or sentences. For e.g.

তুমি ভাত খালানে নাই মই নাজানোঁ । (I do not know whether you have eaten rice or not)

This sentence can be split up into-

মই নাজানোঁ । (I do not know)

তুমি ভাত খালানে ? (Have you eaten rice?)

In Assamese, the same question pattern may be asked in different forms. The pattern may be different, but the meaning of the question remains same. Let us consider the following two examples to understand this.

ৰীণাই কি খাই ভাল পায় ?

কি খাই ভাল পায় ৰীণাই ?

In this way, different question patterns generate the same semantic structure as well as same answer set.

We can also cite the example of rhetorical question where the answer is implicit in the question itself. Although asked in the form of a question, but the semantic structure generates the implicit answer. Such question patterns are basically used in Assamese to enhance the literary quality of Assamese language.

5.2 Proposed Model:

The proposed model for question-answering based on structured representation works in the following way.

Suppose we have the following Assamese sentence -

ৰীণাই আম খাই ভাল পায় (In English, Rina likes to eat mango)

This sentence can be represented in terms of structured text as given below-

Event-1

Instance -	খা	(To eat)
Tense-	বৰ্তমান	(Present)
Agent-	ৰীণা	(Rina)
Object-	আম	(Mango)

Event-2

Instance -	পা	(To get)
Tense-	বৰ্তমান	(Present)
Modifier-	ভাল	(Like)

Again suppose, we want a response to the question-

রীণাই কি খাই ভাল পায় ? (What does Rina like to eat?)

The answer should be - আম (Mango)

To get the answer, we again have to convert the question into structured form [1]. The structured text for the question is represented as follows-

Event-1

Instance -	খা	(To eat)
Tense-	বৰ্তমান	(Present)
Agent-	ৰীণা	(Rina)
* Object-	কি	(What)

Event-2

Instance -	পা	(To get)
Tense-	বৰ্তমান	(Present)
Modifier-	ভাল	(Like)

The part of the structure serving as the answer should be marked. Often these markers correspond to the question words "who" or "what" in the sentence [1]. This structured text for the question will be matched against the structured text generated above. The response is generated based on the segments of the structured text that match the segments of the structured question being asked.

Similarly, the same sentence (as above) can be considered to represent knowledge using logical formalism also. For this, we have to take into consideration the parse tree generated (as in P7) for that sentence. Using this tree structure, logical rules can be derived. These rules of inference can then be used perceive answers to questions. Basically, the representation of rules can be done using First Order Predicate Logic. According to the parse tree, the logical rules of the sentence would be-

S -> NP VP

NP -> PN | CN

VP -> NP VP | AUXV VP | ADJ V

PN -> ৰীণাই

CN -> আম

AUXV -> খাই

ADJ -> ভাল

V -> পায়

As PROLOG structure, the tree can be represented as follows-

S (NP(PN(ৰীণাই)), VP(NP(CN(আম)), VP(AUXV(খাই), VP(ADJ(ভাল), V(পায়)))))

Similarly, if the same question (as above) is asked, then the question may also be transformed into a similar logical representation as shown above. It would be like as follows-

?- S (NP(PN(ৰীণাই)), VP(NP(X), VP(AUXV(খাই), VP(ADJ(ভাল), V(পায়)))))
Then the answer to the question representing the value of X is returned as - আম (Mango)
In this way, we can generate answers to questions from a given set of predicate logic statements using matching process [2].

The structures generated using these two representations may pave the way for doing similar kind of research in other languages also. Languages like Bangali, Oriya or Hindi fall into the category of Indo-Aryan group of languages to which Assamese language also belongs. Therefore, tools developed for one language may help in generating similar kind of tools for other related languages also.

6. Conclusion:

Natural Language Processing has been a significant area of research in recent years. Digital revolution is penetrating in the grassroots level facilitating social development in a faster way. Assamese is a new language for digital revolution. Research works have started for design and development of tools and technologies for this language. Our proposed work will facilitate the preprocessing phase of NLP research in Assamese language. Basically, we have planned to work on syntactic level analysis which will help in automatic knowledge acquisition in terms of linguistics. Our project is the first ever intended work for giving structured and logical representations in Assamese language. As the language is becoming richer for digital revolution, newer applications are becoming possibilities for future understanding of the unexplored areas as well as intricacies of Assamese language. I visualize this work will also pave the way for Artificial Intelligence research works in this language.

References:

[1] Rich Elain, Knight Kevin (1991). *Artificial Intelligence*, Tata McGraw Hill, New Delhi.

[2] Bratko Ivan. *PROLOG Programming for Artificial Intelligence*, Pearson Education.

[3] Chowdhury Gobida G. "*Natural Language Processing*". http://www.cis.strath.ac.uk/cis/research/publications/papers/strath_cis_publication_320.pdf

[4] http://www.cnlp.org/publications/03nlp.lis.encyclopedia.pdf.

[5] Stanojevic Mladen, Vranes Sanja. "*Representation of Texts in Structured Form*". http://www.comsis.org/archive.php?show=ppr275-1009

[6] Costantini Stefania, Florio Niva, Paolucci Alessio. "*A framework for structured knowledge extraction and representation from natural language via deep sentence analysis*". *ceur-ws.org/Vol-810/paper-l18.**pdf***

[7] Bora Lilabati S.(2006). "*Asomia Bhasar Rupatattwa*", Banalata, Panbajar.

[8] Goswami Golak C. (2008). "*Asomia Byakoronor Moulik Bisar*", Bina Library, Guwahati.

[9] Sarma Kr. Shikhar, Gogoi Moromi, Saikia Utpal, Medhi Rakesh. "Foundation and Structure of Developing an Assamese Wordnet" http://www.cfilt.iitb.ac.in/gwc2010/pdfs/50_Assamese_Wordnet__Sarma.pdf

Towards a thematic role based target identification model for question answering

Rivindu Perera[1] *Udayangi Perera*[1]
(1) Informatics Institute of Technology, Colombo 06, Sri Lanka
rivindu.perera@hotmail.com, udayangi@iit.ac.lk

ABSTRACT

Target identification plays a crucial role in web based question answering. But still current approaches are not matured enough to extract the exact target of any given question and therefore leads the system to low precision. To address this gap in the current researches we propose thematic role based methodology to extract the target type of the question. Proposed solution is fully wrapped in the shallow semantic processing of the question rather directing it to the deep parsing. Research employs dative alternation of the question thus providing strict rule based approaches to be implemented to elicit the target with high confidence. Furthermore, the proposed solution can be extended with semantically rich target types by mapping concepts identified in question to semantic categories. This extensibility exhibits that our new approach is scalable and can be tweaked to achieve high precision level that current methods are incapable to achieve.

KEYWORDS: Question answering, target identification, shallow semantic processing, thematic roles

---

1 Introduction

Question answering is the process of extracting the exact answer for a natural language inspired query which usually lies in the Natural Language Processing (NLP) and the Information Retrieval (IR) domains. To extract the answer with high precision, target of the question must be identified in pre-processing stages. Current approaches used in target identification are based on pattern matching approaches and rule based approaches identified through the usage (Shtok et al., 2012). But drawback noticed in this approach is that such techniques cannot be extended with semantically analyzed structures for target identification.

Due to absence of semantic structures in target identification, question answering process may be subjected to several unseen issues during answer extraction. Among these issues, inability to extract the answer though there is enough information in knowledge base is considered as one of the critical issue to be fixed in future question answering. This issue is placed in even more complex stage when question taxonomies are developed with the use of learning process which extracts question target types while processing questions formed by users (Hartrumpf, 2006). Furthermore, inaccurate target identification can also lead the question answering systems to formulate incorrect answer patterns when presenting the final answer for the user thus leading them to have low confidence rates.

Therefore, we propose a solution where target identification in question answering is powered by identified thematic roles in questions. We design our heuristic in a way that future researches can also incorporate the method by extending the structure with any thematic role that need to be incorporated.

To evaluate this new paradigm we have used Scholar - question answering system (Perera, 2012) which is designed with the proposed target identification method by this research. This paper will unwrap all steps taken to develop this novel method with an empirical viewpoint of each and every approach we have employed during implementation.

2 Background of the study

2.1 Target identification in question answering

Bilotti and Nyberg (Bilotti and Nyberg, 2008) argue that question answering can be taken in to a level that can challenge human abilities only through a better extraction technique which can get the exact answer for the given query. However, in their research which warps around the OpenEphyra question answering system, shows that passage ranking is not the most important task in question answering. Ramakrishnan et al. (Ramakrishnan et al., 2003) also support this concept showing that high quality answer can only be extracted through the proper understanding of the target required by the end user. But Whittaker et al. (Whittaker et al., 2006) bring out that factoid question answering cannot be implemented with a pre-processed set of target types which can be selected by the end user rather this research shows the importance of dynamic target type identification in answer extraction can lead question answering systems to be more flexible and useful when such systems are used in open domain question answering.

Kato et al. (Kato et al., 2006) show a practical target identification method using 4 different target types which are responsible to generate answers using categorization of answer type. Table

1 below, shows the syntactic classification of user utterances and its distribution found by Kato and his team.

Syntactic form	
Wh-type Question	87.7% (544)
Yes-no Question	9.5% (59)
Imperative (Information request)	2.6% (16)
Declarative (Answer to clarification)	0.2% (1)

Table 1: Syntactic classification of user utterances from (Kato et al., 2006)

According to these findings it is noted that Wh-type questions are the main type of questions that any particular question answering systems should be able to answer. But this type of a distribution cannot be considered as accurate in all the scenarios that must be handled through a open domain question answering system. Sacaleanu & Neumann (Sacaleanu and Neumann, 2006) show that in cross-language question answering, target of the question cannot be determined by simple rule based approach rather need to be analysed thoroughly through semantically rich aspects.

2.2 Thematic roles

Pighin et al. (Pighin et al., 2007) introduce a two-steps supervised strategy for the identification and classification of thematic roles. In this approach presented by Pighin and his team, wide variety of themes are considered providing better overview of the recognition of thematic roles and classification in a complex and wide area of natural text. However this research does not employ the verb sense information in classification stage. Therefore, in a question answering system this approach cannot be used with original structure as question answering needs verbs to be defined with high precision considering the sense they provide.

Liu and Soo (Liu and Soo, 1993) carried out a research in the area of knowledge acquisition considering thematic role based approach. In this novel method proposed and evaluated by this research, syntactic clues are incorporated to get the exact role to the acquisition phase. But the drawback noticed in this research is that need of extensive syntactic resources to determine the knowledge to be acquired. Therefore when applied to a question answering system this method should be trained with large amount data to make this heuristic available for all sorts of questions.

3 Method

In our approach target identification is entirely based on the thematic role identified which shows the type of the answer to be extracted. This novel paradigm is also inspired from the research carried out by Yang et al. (Yang et al., 2006) which introduces contextual question answering using relevancy recognition. But to transform this question answering process to a flexible state we also introduce the method that users are given the chance to select the thematic role that they need. However, if such thematic role is absence terms used in the question, its structure and the semantic representation are considered to extract the thematic role.

3.1 Thematic role identification

In the target identification process the first task is to identify the thematic role to be identified which later transformed in to a target type. In our approach, seven different thematic roles are incorporated and these are listed in Table 2 with their applicability in the question context. These thematic roles are inspired from the seminal work carried out by Jurafsky & Martin (Jurafsky and Martin, 2000).

Thematic role	Applicability
Agent	To get the agent role of a question. This may incorporate any object type if specified object is involved in the act playing the role of agent. Ex: *Who* found the Google?
Instrument	If the question is related with an event, instruments used in the event are classified under this role What is the *chemical substance* he used to make NaOH?
Goal	Goal thematic role can show any type of a objective such as a location, event or some other result which is carried out to invoke a different type of an event To *where* he travelled?
Patient	Object type of a event is categorized under this thematic role Ex: What *company* did Sergy Brin start?
Beneficiary	Beneficiary of a question is the person or thing that gets some benefit from the event. For *whom* he made the aircraft?
Source	When questions are associated with transfer events, then origin of the subjected object is considered as source. *Where* did he come from?
Result	When questions are associated with result of an event. Ex: *What* did he build?

Table 2: Thematic roles

To identify the thematic role of a question, we employ rule based approach determined by the considered set of thematic roles. As the first task question is represented in a tagged form using Hidden Markov Model (HMM) tagger. Reason behind to use this stochastic tagging procedure is that HMM tagger selects the best sequence of tags for the entire question processed(Jurafsky and Martin, 2000). Basically, bigram-HMM tagger we employed will therefore assign the tag considering the sequence as a whole as expressed in fundamental theorem in (1),

$$t_i = \arg\max_j P(t_j | t_{i-1}) P(w_i | t_j) \tag{1}$$

where t_i represents current tag to be determined and w_i as the current word considered. But we have also considered several other approaches like Brill tagging as well. But earlier mentioned reason inspired us to utilize this HMM tagging. Tagged question is used to invoke the basic analysis of the structure of the question. But our main task of thematic role assignment is done via predefined model which consume the tagged question to map the appropriate model. Simply, once question is tagged with appropriate tag sets, it is easy identify what lexical context it represents as a formal description is available for the question. This formal description is used to select the thematic role from predefined collection of thematic role to abstract formal description matching. Once the thematic role is identified it is associated with the specified question to support the answer extraction process.

3.2 Thematic role assignment and metadata processing

Identified thematic role will be assigned to the specified question showcasing the answer type required to be extracted. But with the thematic role several other metadata can also be attached to the question to make the answer extraction process more accurate and fast. If thematic role required represent any type of supported named entity them the named entity type will also be attached to the question. For an example for a question like “who is the founder of Google” will be assigned with the “agent” thematic role. But in question processing it can be identified that this agent type is actually mapped to a “person” named entity type. Therefore, rather assigning the generic theme of agent as a metadata representation “person” named entity will also be attached to the question to support answer extraction by reducing the search space. We currently consider six such types of named entities in our approach, person, location, currency, city, date and organization.

3.3 Answer extraction

When the thematic role is assigned to a question, answer extraction process can be stated focusing answers which represent the type required by the thematic role and which are compatible with the named entity type specified. After the extraction process, confidence level can be assigned to the extracted answer by analyzing the compatibility that answer carries with thematic role and metadata associated with the question being processed.

4 Results and discussion

To evaluate the proposed novel approach, we employ 280 questions from past TREC (Voorhees, 2001) series (TREC-8 and TREC-9). We manually categorized these 280 questions into 7 main classes representing all major thematic roles we are defining in this research. Important factor we have noticed is that for some thematic roles, population of questions is not sufficient. But as TREC is defining its own standard of question formulation and as future researches in the same track need to compare result with our approach, we have used the original collection without adding our own questions to populate classes with fewer questions.

Question class based on thematic role	With correct target	With incorrect target	Correctly answered
Agent	68	3	62
Instrument	58	6	51
Goal	10	9	6
Patient	51	5	43
Beneficiary	12	3	8
Source	23	1	22
Result	24	7	17
Total	246	34	219

Table 3: Evaluation result using TREC question set

Table 3 expresses the result of evaluation expressing three factors, the number of questions with correctly identified targets, the number of questions with incorrectly identified targets and number of questions where correct answers are acquired using identified thematic role.

According to the evaluation results it is noted that systems have achieved 78.20% average accuracy level considering correctly answered questions. When comparing with other systems which are tested with same TREC question sets it can be determined that this accuracy level is better than such system have achieved (Zheng, 2002) (Voorhees, 2003). But importantly it can be noticed that error rate of target identification is lying in the 12.14% which is quite acceptable and therefore shows high accuracy level in target identification.

Though our approach has shown excellent accuracy as an average rate, it can be clearly identified that for some individual thematic roles, low accuracy levels are also displayed. According to our preliminary analysis of this behaviour several reasons are uncovered. Firstly, target identification greatly depends on the steady structure of the questions. This encompasses that if question structure is leading to the answer, for an example through agent type or patient type, then it is easy to assign thematic role rather mining it deeper. Furthermore, it is found that short questions which can be directly formed into a grammatical representation can ended up with high accuracy levels in thematic role assignment.

5 Conclusion and future work

In this paper we illustrated an approach to determine the target type of a question by analyzing the thematic role of the question to be processed. As thematic roles are based on the semantic representation of the natural text this approach can be extended to support several semantic processing tasks. Furthermore, in several stages we have employed rule based approaches to process the question as probabilistic approaches cannot be applied with semantic representation with high accuracy.

To evaluate this novel heuristic we have used the question answering system- Scholar which uses the same strategy to identify the target. During evaluation we achieved excellent accuracy which inspires us to develop this model as an independent library to incorporate with other question answering systems. In future our focus is entirely placed on the implementation of this heuristic as a library and to apply several other semantic processing methodologies to increase the accuracy level of this novel paradigm.

References

Bilotti, M.W., Nyberg, E., 2008. Improving text retrieval precision and answer accuracy in question answering systems, Coling 2008: Proceedings of the 2nd workshop on Information Retrieval for Question Answering. Association for Computational Linguistics, Manchester, UK, pp. 1-8.

Hartrumpf, S., 2006. Adapting a semantic question answering system to the web, Proceedings of the Workshop on Multilingual Question Answering. Association for Computational Linguistics, pp. 61-68.

Jurafsky, D., Martin, J.H., 2000. Speech and Language Processing: An Introduction to Natural Language Processing, Computational Linguistics, and Speech Recognition. Prentice Hall PTR.

Kato, T., Masui, F., Fukumoto, J.i., Kando, N., 2006. WoZ simulation of interactive question answering, Proceedings of the Interactive Question Answering Workshop at HLT-NAACL 2006. Association for Computational Linguistics, New York City, NY, pp. 9-16.

Liu, R.-L., Soo, V.-W., 1993. An empirical study on thematic knowledge acquisition based on syntactic clues and heuristics, Proceedings of the 31st annual meeting on Association for Computational Linguistics. Association for Computational Linguistics, Columbus, Ohio, pp. 243-250.

Perera, R., 2012. Scholar: Cognitive Computing Approach for Question Answering, Department of Computer Science, Informatics Institute of Technology. University of Westminster.

Pighin, D., Moschitti, A., Basili, R., 2007. RTV: tree kernels for thematic role classification, Proceedings of the 4th International Workshop on Semantic Evaluations. Association for Computational Linguistics, Prague, Czech Republic, pp. 288-291.

Ramakrishnan, G., Jadhav, A., Joshi, A., Chakrabarti, S., Bhattacharyya, P., 2003. Question Answering via Bayesian inference on lexical relations, Proceedings of the ACL 2003 workshop on Multilingual summarization and question answering - Volume 12. Association for Computational Linguistics, Sapporo, Japan, pp. 1-10.

Sacaleanu, B., Neumann, G., 2006. Cross-cutting aspects of cross-language question answering systems, Proceedings of the Workshop on Multilingual Question Answering. Association for Computational Linguistics, pp. 15-22.

Shtok, A., Dror, G., Maarek, Y., Szpektor, I., 2012. Learning from the past: answering new questions with past answers, Proceedings of the 21st international conference on World Wide Web. ACM, Lyon, France, pp. 759-768.

Voorhees, E.M., 2001. Question answering in TREC, Proceedings of the tenth international conference on Information and knowledge management. ACM, Atlanta, Georgia, USA, pp. 535-537.

Voorhees, E.M., 2003. Evaluating the evaluation: a case study using the TREC 2002 question answering track, Proceedings of the 2003 Conference of the North American Chapter of the Association for Computational Linguistics on Human Language Technology - Volume 1. Association for Computational Linguistics, Edmonton, Canada, pp. 181-188.

Whittaker, E.W.D., Hamonic, J., Yang, D., Klingberg, T., Furui, S., 2006. Monolingual web-based factoid question answering in Chinese, Swedish, English and Japanese, Proceedings of the Workshop on Multilingual Question Answering. Association for Computational Linguistics, pp. 45-52.

Yang, F., Feng, J., Fabbrizio, G.D., 2006. A data driven approach to relevancy recognition for contextual question answering, Proceedings of the Interactive Question Answering Workshop at HLT-NAACL 2006. Association for Computational Linguistics, New York City, NY, pp. 33-40.

Zheng, Z., 2002. AnswerBus question answering system, Proceedings of the second international conference on Human Language Technology Research. Morgan Kaufmann Publishers Inc., San Diego, California, pp. 399-404.

Assessment of Answers: Online Subjective Examination

Asmita Dhokrat[1,] *Gite Hanumant R*[2,] *C.Namrata Mahender*[3]
(1) (2) (3) DEPT. OF .COMPUTER SCIENCE AND INFORMATION TECHNOLOGY,
Dr. Babasaheb Ambedkar Marathwada University, Aurangabad, MS, India
asmita.dhokrat@gmail.com, hanumantgitecsit@gmail.com,
nam.mah@gmail.com

ABSTRACT

Question answering is a specified form of information retrieval. Our work comes under closed domain question answering. We are working on assessment of answer for online subjective examination. Examination and evaluation are part of every course module so are even in online examination, objective based examination are already available but subjective examination are in need of time as subjective assessment is considered as best way of evaluation of ones subject understanding & knowledge. In our paper we have discussed two issues related to the answer method i.e. length & paraphrasing. And have obtained a pattern extraction by creating a sequence for a given answer. Our system has a centralized file system which includes the reference material as well as the model answer for questions. These are used for matching and evaluating a candidate's answer. For every correct answer a confidence factor of being positive is assigned when the required selective pattern of candidates answer matches with the model answer.

KEYWORDS: Online Subjective Examination, Paraphrase, Evaluation process

1 Question Answering

Question Answering is a specialized form of information retrieval. Given a collection of documents, a Question Answering system attempts to retrieve correct answers to questions posed in natural language.

Open-domain question answering requires question answering systems to be able to answer questions about any conceivable topic. Such systems cannot, therefore, rely on hand crafted domain specific knowledge to find and extract the correct answers.

Closed-domain question answering deals with questions under a specific domain (for example, medicine or automotive maintenance), and can be seen as an easier task because NLP systems can exploit domain-specific knowledge frequently formalized in ontologies. Alternatively, closed-domain might refer to a situation where only a limited type of questions are accepted, such as questions asking for descriptive rather than procedural information. Our system also comes under closed domain QA where we are supposed for accessing online based subjective examination.

2 Subjective Examination

Subjective examination has been a major way of evaluating a candidate's knowledge & understanding about on course or subject in traditional education system for centuries (Minsu Jang et al. 2007). Every university has its own examination pattern based on subjective examination. So in this global era of web based education. We need to consider such examination done online (Hanumant R. Gite, C.Namrata Mahender 2012).

Generally the questions may be considered in the following forms.

- Define: explain the meaning and (often) provide an appropriate example
- Describe / illustrate: present the main points with clear examples that enhance the discussion
- Differentiate / distinguish: present the differences between two things
- Discuss / explain: present the main points, facts, and details of a topic; give reasons
- Enumerate / List / Identify / Outline: write a list of the main points with brief explanations
- Interpret: present your analysis of the topic using facts and reasoning
- Justify / Prove: present evidence and reasons that support the topic
- Summarize: briefly state the main ideas in an organized manner
- Trace: state the main points in logical or chronological order

In this paper we have discussed two issues related to examination & a simple Psycho based solution is provided.

3 Online Subjective Examination

Our system works on an attempt to consider candidates answer by extracting the required intentional part of an answer to a prescribed template or model answer already provided in the Question answering framework.

There is always an urge to justify an answer is appropriate or not. That is we have to find the confidence level for a given answer, by comparing it to the model answer. That is every word in an answer does not play an important role while evaluation process. To justify such case we have consider answer in one sentence.

3.1 Question Processing Module

- The question type, usually based on a taxonomy of possible questions already coded into the system;
- The expected answer type, through some shallow semantic processing of the question; and
- The question focus, which represents the main information that is required to answer the user's question.

These steps allow the question processing module to finally pass a set of query terms to the Paragraph Indexing module, which uses them to perform the information retrieval.

3.2 Answer Processing

The Answer Processing module is responsible for identifying and extracting the emphasized words which are responsible for the response of the answer.

3.2.1 Answer Identification

The use of a part-of-speech tagger (e.g., Python POS tagger) can help to enable recognition of answer candidates within identified model answer. Answer candidates can be ranked based on measures of distance between keywords, numbers of keywords matched and other similar heuristic metrics.

3.2.2 Answer Extraction

Once an answer has been identified, the shallow parsing performed is leveraged to extract only the relevant word or phrase in answer to the question.

3.2.3 Answer Correctness

Confidence in the correctness of an answer can be increased in a number of ways. One way is to use a lexical resource like WordNet (Synonyms) to verify that a candidate response was of the correct answer type.

3.3 One line answer

In our system we are paying attention for answer accessing majorly by considering length and paraphrasing. One line answer or Define may have a sentence which may have 10 words or 15 words as per the writing style of the candidates so we cannot fix single line answer with fixed number of words used. So only point to be find single sentence is to find the full stop.

For e.g. one line answer, expressed in different mode or synonym based answer etc. (where s is stands for original and t is for its paraphrase)

- s. Tom purchased a Honda from John.
- t. Tom bought a Honda from John.
- s. It was a Honda that John sold to Tom.

- t. John sold a Honda to Tom.
- s. Tom bought a Honda from John.
- t. John sold a Honda to Tom(Atsushi Fujita 2005)

Answer can be stated in an 'n' way but few words only have intended meaning for the particular answer. Some issues in such answer.

- Such words may have replaced by its synonyms.
- The sentence is paraphrased.

For considering a bit more complexity of an answer we have also performed processing on multiline answer. Here the reflection or impact of paraphrasing can be seen more clearly.

3.4 Multi line answer

Same case is with answer the question is detail or Brief. We cannot fix the size of paragraphs or pages. Generally a restriction of words will be provided so every answer has to be in the given length, but still there is a huge range for example single sentence answers we may say can have almost 20 words i.e. we can answer it with a single word to 20 words and all are valid, only more than 20 words will not be considered as desirable answer.

E.g. what does distributed operating system manages?

- A distributed operating system manages a group of independent computers and makes them appear to be a single computer.
- A distributed operating system handles a set of autonomous computer also makes them emerge to be a single system.
- A set of independent systems are integrated to make them appear to be single computer.

3.5 Paraphrasing

In our work may be single line answering or multiline following points in paraphrasing are focused during the evaluating process.

Paraphrasing (synonym based, lexical / structural based, alteration based)

- Paraphrasing of common nouns to their synonyms
- Paraphrasing of common nouns to their definition statements
- Paraphrasing of verbs to their synonyms
- Paraphrasing of verbs to their definition statements

We are paying more focus on the intention answer compared to the focus of question. We tend towards the expected answer as per the requirement of the focused issue or the object. Following table 1 shows the focused or intended portion or words in a few answers in our system.

Question No.	Keywords	Right answer	Wrong Answer
Q1	manages/handle computer/CPU/processor/system between/among user/client	5	5
Q2	Quick/fast/rapid/ immediate Predictable/knowable Response/reply/ reaction/ answer Events/action	8	2
Q3	group/cluster/set independent/self computer/CPU/processor/system make/create/build appear/become visible/show single/distinct computer/CPU/processor/system	8	2
Q4	Program/ agenda/ plan in/during execution/ finishing/ completion	10	0
Q5	some/few/various/several event/result/occurrence/interrupt occur/happen/takes place	7	3
Q6	some/few/various/several process/procedure/course/method running/executes at/by/on all/every utilization/use/operation	6	4
Q7	select/few/various/several processes/procedure/course/method queues/row/line	7	3
Q8	compact/solid extremely/very/tremendously efficient/capable/able by/via/through design/plan/intend	3	7

TABLE 1 – Answers with emphasized words

4 Representation of intended answer

A question can be assumed in many ways as per the candidate understanding and the strength of vocabulary plus the expressive nature of the candidate. As an answer to be correct can take any form but the intended meaning should not change, the way of answers are paraphrased for an intended answer for representing the importance of word in a particular answer and the number of ways of answering, we have chosen a simple state transition diagram to represent the answer, for e.g. following question

Question:-

What is main objective of real time operating system?

Has such expected answer as per the reference material provided.

Answer:-

1. Quick predictable response to events.
2. Return correct result within time constraints.
3. Responds to input instantly.
4. Response time very short.

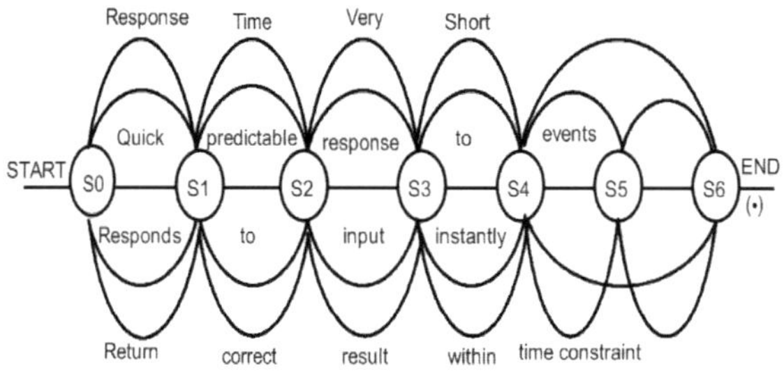

FIGURE 1– State transition diagram

5 Our system

The candidates are taken as a text file and separately stored under a folder which is unique for each candidate.

We maintain a centralized file system where the reference materials and the model answer for each question is kept.

5.1 The Evaluation process

The candidate answer is first extracted from the file and a sequence state transition is generated i.e. nothing but a state transition diagram using the given input for example.

As we have conducted exam on ten candidates for twelve questions, we had a verity of cases to adhere the paraphrased answer.

In general the process start with POS tree along with sequence extraction of the candidate answer which is compared with the model answer.

If exact terms are found in candidates answer as per the model answer & its key terms it is evaluated as correct else we try to find the key terms which are there in the model answer and are part of candidates answer then its semantic analysis is done using a word net dictionary that provides the density of each word in a given sequence, if that get a match for more than 50% words in a sentence it is also termed as correct else declared as wrong.

This density of words are keywords of the answer which are stored in our key terms those are the words which are given high confidence so that they are to be considers as positive words to reflect the correct meaning to the answer.

A sample answer of 10 candidates is given in table 2 for the question "When the process does goes into waiting state?"

Candidate. No.	Candidate Answer	Answer Right/ Wrong	Reason
1	When the execution time of process gets complete the process goes to waiting state.	Wrong	Meaning Change
2	When some events to occur after running state then process go in waiting state.	Right	--
3	When process is ready to execution and it has to wait for some event then it goes to waiting state.	Right	--
4	The processes go in waiting state. When for some event to occur such as an I/O completion or reception of a signal.	Right	--
5	When process is in running as some ***intrupt*** are created then process is waiting state.	Wrong	Spell Mistake
	After automatically correcting using Word Net dictionary	Right	Correct
6	The process is waiting for some event to occur [I/O completion or reception of a signal]	Right	--
7	The process go in waiting for some events to occur (such as I/O completion or reception of a signal)	Right	--
8	Waiting for some events to occur.	Right	
9	---	Wrong	Not Attempted
10	A process executes it changes state as we know that process task. As if process is executed and process is waiting for some events to occur then we can say that the process is in waiting state.	Right	--

TABLE 2 – Paraphrased answer for given question.

From 10 candidates stated, three were wrong. Candidate 1 answer was incorrect due to semantically be different from the model answer, while a Candidate 5 answer has spell mistakes. But using word net option it can be automating corrected by providing semantically same answer and candidate 9 has not attempted the answer thus to be taken as wrong answer.

For verifying the answer for its appropriateness a confidence factor was provided for each answer, as per the sequence of pattern match found between the candidate and model answer. If the density of matching is more than or equal to 50% then the answer was termed to be correct and it is known as positive confidence else a negative confidence is provide for the mismatched and the answer is termed to be wrong.

Following table 3 shows the confidence factor for the evaluated answer.

Q No.	Model Answer	Right Answer	Wrong Answer	Positive confidence	Negative confidence
Q.1	Software that handles computer hardware, Intermediator between user hardware,	5	5	50%	50%
Q.2	quick predictable response to events	8	2	80%	20%
Q.3	Group independent computers make them appear to single computer	8	2	80%	20%
Q.4	A process is a the unit of work in a system, Process is a program in execution	10	0	100%	0%
Q.5	The process is waiting for some event to occur	7	3	70%	30%
Q.6	Some process running at all times to maximize CPU utilization.	6	4	60%	40%
Q.7	Job, ready, device, waiting, i/o, priority	6	4	60%	40%
Q.8	Selecting processes from these queues, A process is migrates between various scheduling queues throughout its lifetime.	8	2	80%	20%
Q.9	Windows CE, Minix 3	10	0	100%	0%
Q.10	Interrupts	10	0	100%	0%
Q.11	Compact and efficient by design, They are designed to operate on small machines like PDAs with less autonomy.	7	3	70%	30%
Q.12	Kernel	9	0	90%	10%

TABLE 3 – Answers with confidence level

In our sample set of questions descriptive and describe type of questions were not considered. The overall efficiency of evaluation for our sample set was found to be 70%.

Conclusion

Online subjective examination is need of time. It is too complex due to the expressive power, vocabulary used and understanding of the subject is involved of every individual and all this causes large variations in the writing style of an answer person to person. Thus variation of length words, form of sentence all matters while evaluating the answer. Online examination is a type of closed domain question answering as it limited to course applied. In our work we have focused on the intended part of answer required to verify a particular answer as correct. Word has great emphasis in our system, POS tagging was also performed while extraction of words for better accuracy.

Overall performance of our system was found to be 70%. Major constraint of our system is brief, short note, described in detail, discussed type of question including mathematical formulas, diagrams, examples were not considering as a part of question answering.

References

Atsushi Fujita(2005), *Automatic Generation of Syntactically Well-formed and Semantically Appropriate Paraphrases,* Doctoral thesis submitted at Department of Information Processing, Graduate School of Information Science, Nara Institute of Science and Technology March 2005

Hanumant R. Gite, C.Namrata Mahender (2012), *Representation of Model Answer: Online Subjective Examination System,* National conference NC3IT2012 Sinhgad, Institute of Computer Sciences Pandharpur.

Minsu Jang, Joo-Chan Sohn, Hyun Kyu Cho(2007), *Automated Question Answering using Semantic Web Services,* IEEE Asia-Pacific Services Computing Conference. 2007

Yuan, Zhenming, et al.(2006), *A Web-Based Examination and Evaluation System for Computer Education*, Washington, DC: IEEE Computer Society, 2006

WikiTalk: A Spoken Wikipedia-based Open-Domain Knowledge Access System

Graham WILCOCK
UNIVERSITY OF HELSINKI, Finland
graham.wilcock@helsinki.fi

ABSTRACT
WikiTalk is an open-domain knowledge access system that talks about topics using Wikipedia articles as its knowledge source. Based on Constructive Dialogue Modelling theory, WikiTalk exploits the concepts of Topic and NewInfo to manage topic-tracking and topic-shifting. As the currently talked-about Topic can be any Wikipedia topic, the system is truly open-domain. NewInfos, the pieces of new information to be conveyed to the partner, are associated with hyperlinks extracted from the Wikipedia texts. Using these hyperlinks the system can change topics smoothly according to the user's changing interests. As well as user-initiated topics, the system can suggest new topics using for example the daily "Did you know?" items in Wikipedia. WikiTalk can be employed in different environments. It has been demonstrated on Windows, with an open-source robotics simulator, and with the Aldebaran Nao humanoid robot.

KEYWORDS: Open-domain knowledge access, spoken dialogue system, Wikipedia, human-robot interaction.

1 Introduction

The paper describes WikiTalk, an open-domain knowledge access system that talks about topics using Wikipedia articles as its knowledge source. The system is truly open-domain in the sense that the currently talked-about topic can be any topic that Wikipedia has an article about, and the user can switch topics at any time and as often as desired.

In an open-domain system it is extremely important to keep track of the current topic and to have smooth mechanisms for changing to new topics. In WikiTalk, topic-tracking and topic-shifting are managed with the help of the concepts of Topic and NewInfo, in accordance with the Constructive Dialogue Modelling theory of Jokinen (2009). The distinctive contribution of WikiTalk is that NewInfos, the pieces of new information to be conveyed to the partner, are associated with hyperlinks extracted from the Wikipedia texts. Using these hyperlinks the system can change topics smoothly according to the human's changing interests.

Interaction technology has to address the engagement of the user in the interaction. The system has to manage the interaction so that there is a natural conversation rather than a monologue on a particular topic. For instance, in teaching and learning situations such conversational capability is important. This requires dynamic tracking not only of dialogue topics but also of the users' focus of attention and of the user's level of interest in the topic. Techniques for attention-tracking and interest-tracking in interactive situations are important parts of the system.

WikiTalk has been developed so that it can be integrated into different hardware and software environments. In spoken human-computer interaction scenarios, such as a hands-free in-car conversational companion, WikiTalk requires suitable speech recognition and speech synthesis components. The system can be used on Windows, using the standard Windows Speech Engine components. In embodied agent scenarios, for example in human-robot interaction, the system needs to be integrated with appropriate multimodal components for face-tracking, nodding and gesturing, proximity recognition and so on.

An extended version of WikiTalk has been implemented on the Aldebaran Nao robot, as the basis for multimodal human-robot conversational interaction (Jokinen and Wilcock, 2012b; Csapo et al., 2012). We are not aware of any previously-reported multimodal human-robot conversational interaction system that is open-domain.

The paper is structured as follows. Section 2 presents background on dialogue modelling and human-robot interaction. Section 3 introduces the basic approach to implementing open-domain dialogues using Wikipedia. Section 4 describes how smooth topic shifts are handled. Section 5 presents an example open-domain conversation with a robot. Section 6 considers related work and Section 7 describes multimodal extensions for humanoid robots.

2 Dialogue Modelling and Human-Robot Interaction

The theoretical basis of WikiTalk is Constructive Dialogue Modelling (Jokinen, 2009), which integrates topic management, information flow, and the construction of shared knowledge in the conversation by communicative agents. We have applied this model to human-robot interaction, in which cooperation manifests itself in the system properties that allow users to interact in a natural manner, i.e. in the ways in which the system affords cooperative interaction. The agents' goals can range from rather vague "keep the channel open"-type social goals to more specific, task-oriented goals such as planning a trip, providing information, or giving instructions.

Jokinen and Wilcock (2011) describe different levels of emergent verbal behaviour that arise when speech is used in human-robot interaction. At the first levels of verbal behaviour the robot produces spoken monologues giving a stream of simple explanations of its movements, and the human uses voice commands to direct the robot's movements. At the next level, cooperative verbal behaviour begins to emerge when the robot modifies its own verbal behaviour in response to being asked by the human to talk less or more.

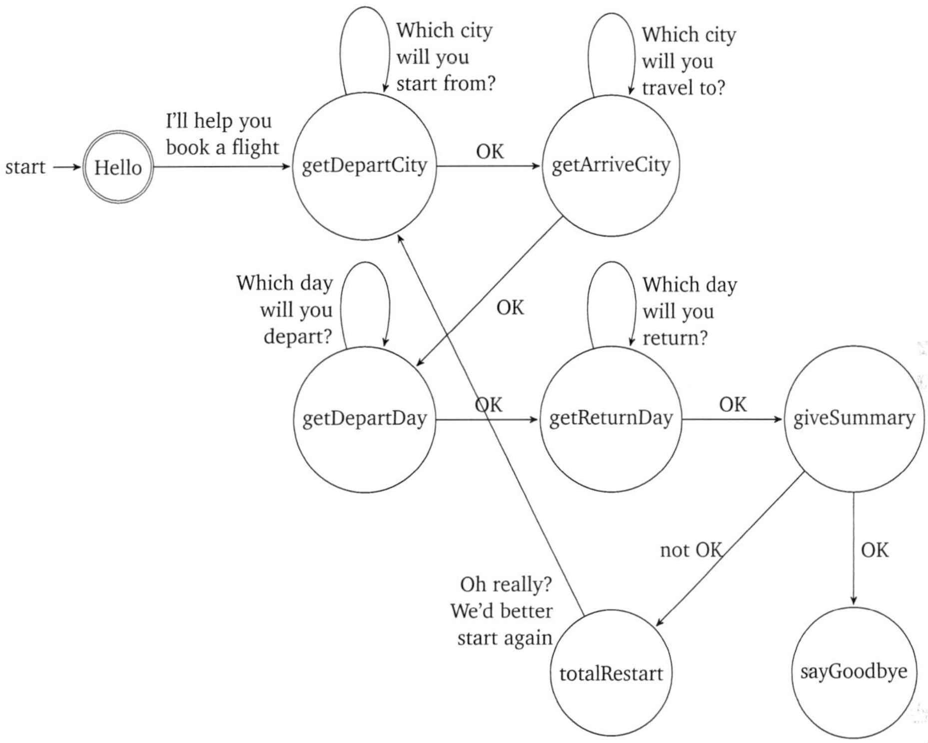

Figure 1: An example finite-state machine for a closed-domain dialogue.

2.1 Closed-Domain Dialogues

Moving up a level, the robot asks questions in order to achieve a specified dialogue goal. The classic example of this kind of dialogue is a flight reservation system. Finite state machines have been successfully used for these closed-domain form-filling dialogues. An example is shown in Figure 1.

Here, the system asks questions in order to achieve the dialogue goal by filling in the required fields in the form. The specific questions are predefined for each specific domain. Although it is easy to change the details about the flights, the destinations and the departure times that are maintained in the system's database, it is very difficult to change to a different domain.

In order to move up another level, to open-domain dialogues, we use Wikipedia as a source of world knowledge. By exploiting ready-made paragraphs and sentences from Wikipedia, WikiTalk enables a robot to talk about an almost infinite range of topics. The robot can also perform smooth topic-shifts according to the human's interests, by using hyperlinks extracted from the Wikipedia articles. As well as human-initiated topics, the robot can suggest new topics using for example the daily "Did you know?" items in Wikipedia.

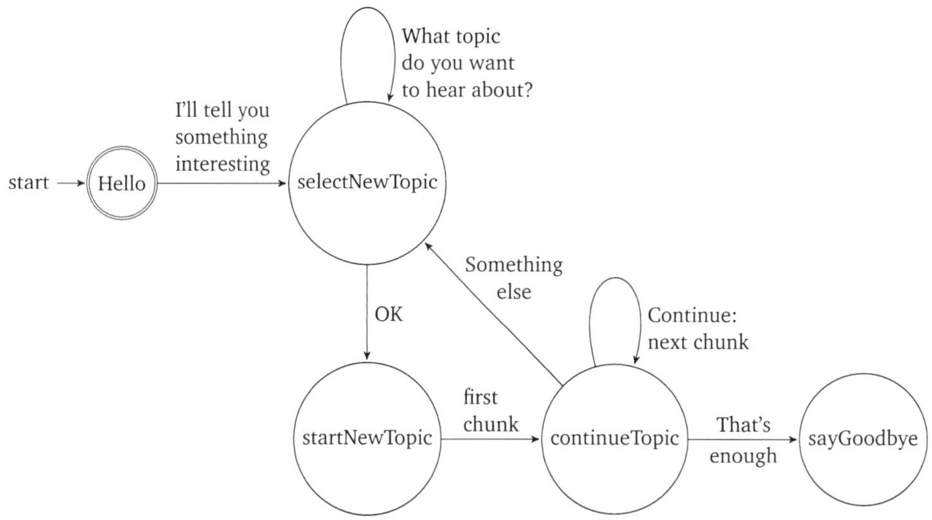

Figure 2: Towards a finite-state machine for open-domain dialogues.

3 Getting Started with Open-Domain Dialogues

In order to support open-domain dialogues, the dialogue control model in WikiTalk is different from the closed-domain form-filling systems. The basic interaction management is still controlled by finite-state transitions, but the set of states are not linked to specific domain-related items such as "get departure day" or "get destination city" in a closed-domain system. Rather, the states are used to manage the flow of the interaction with the user, especially topic-tracking and topic-shifting. This approach makes it possible for a finite number of states to manage dialogues with an infinite number of topics.

The following sections present an introduction to some of the states needed for open-domain dialogues, showing how conversations can be started and stopped, and how topics within a conversation can be started, continued and stopped. A partial diagram of these states is shown in Figure 2

3.1 Hello and Goodbye

Like closed-domain dialogue systems, an open-domain system needs a way to get started and a way to finish. These are handled by a Hello state and a Goodbye state. As well as saying "Hello" and "Goodbye", these states can be extended with suitable behaviours. For example, a mobile robot can stop moving around for the duration of the conversation. A humanoid robot can stand up to talk, or sit down to talk, depending on the scenario.

3.2 Selecting a Topic

After the Hello state, the system moves to the SelectTopic state. There are different ways to select a topic. The easiest way to get started is to select a topic from a list of favourites or from a history list of recently talked-about topics. WikiTalk provides convenient ways to extend the favourites by adding the current topic to the list, and to remind the user about the favourites or the recent history topics. Other ways to select a topic are described in Sections 4.6 and 4.7.

3.3 Starting a New Topic

When a new topic has been selected, the NewTopic state gets the text for the topic from Wikipedia. As Wikipedia articles are designed for visual inspection in web browsers, with visual layouts, footnotes, and various special symbols, a certain amount of cleaning-up and reformatting is necessary to make the text suitable for reading by a speech synthesizer.

In addition, the text is divided into chunks (paragraphs and sentences) of a suitable size for spoken dialogue contributions. The appropriate chunk size depends on several factors. If the system has a good interrupt mechanism (Section 3.5), a large chunk size (whole paragraphs) is fine as the user can easily stop the system talking at any point. Otherwise, a small chunk size (a single sentence) is better, so the system can check frequently between chunks for positive or negative feedback before continuing or stopping.

3.4 Continuing the Same Topic

Once a new topic has been started, the ContinueTopic state manages the system's presentation of the chunks of the topic text. If the user asks for more, or otherwise shows some interest in the topic, the system continues with the next chunk. If the user keeps asking for more until the end of the article is reached, the system says that there is no more information about the current topic and moves to the SelectTopic state (Section 3.2) which asks the user to select a new topic.

At the end of each chunk about a given topic, the user can ask for the same chunk to be repeated, or can ask to go back to the previous chunk about the current topic. The user can also interrupt the current chunk without listening to it all, and ask to skip forward to the next chunk on the same topic.

3.5 Interrupting the System

It is helpful if there is a simple way to interrupt the system while it is talking. Otherwise, the user has to wait until the system finishes the current chunk before telling it to stop. This can be annoying if the system has mistakenly chosen the wrong topic and the chunk size is a whole paragraph.

The best interrupt mechanism depends on the hardware and software environment. Some speech engines support barge-in, others do not. Some robots have a convenient button or sensor that can be used to interrupt the robot's behaviour. In this case, large paragraph-size chunks can be interrupted whenever desired.

When the system is interrupted, it stops talking and moves to an Interrupt state, remembering which state it was in when the interruption occurred, what the topic was, and which chunk it had reached. It explicitly acknowledges the interruption by saying "Oh sorry!" and waiting for the user's input. The user can then tell it to continue, to go back to an earlier chunk, to skip forward to the next chunk, or to switch to a new topic.

4 Enhancements for Open-Domain Dialogues

In natural human-human dialogues, the topic changes dynamically as the conversation goes along. When the topic changes smoothly from the current topic to a related topic, there is no need to make the change of topic explicit. A change to a related topic is normally a smooth topic shift, and this occurs more or less continuously. It is important that dialogue systems have smooth mechanisms to support smooth topic shifts.

4.1 Topic Trees

Previously, dialogue systems have often used topic trees to organize knowledge into related topics. Focus trees (McCoy and Cheng, 1991) were originally proposed to trace foci in natural language generation systems. The branches of the tree show what sort of shifts are cognitively easy to process and can be expected to occur in dialogues. Random jumps from one branch to another are unlikely, and if they do occur, they should be appropriately marked. The tree both constrains and enables prediction of what is likely to be talked about next.

Our approach finds an equivalent to topic trees by exploiting the hyperlinks found in Wikipedia. These links provide a ready-made organisation of domain knowledge, for almost any domain. We believe this approach is better than hand-coding topic trees or automatic clustering. Kirschner (2007) gives an overview of these approaches to Interactive Question Answering. Jokinen et al. (1998) combine a manually built tree for main topics with an n-gram model for topic shifts. Kirschner and Bernardi (2009) use machine learning to explore follow-up questions.

Instead of attempting a deep processing approach involving information extraction, question answering or summarization techniques, we prefer a shallow processing approach in which selected chunks of the Wikipedia texts are read out aloud, with a relatively small amount of reformatting and clean-up necessary for spoken contributions. This shallow approach allows us to concentrate on identifying hyperlinks and on managing the topic shifts smoothly.

4.2 Smooth Topic Shifts

When the system is talking about the current topic, the chunks contain NewInfos, pieces of new information about the current topic. In Wikipedia, these NewInfos are typically annotated with hyperlinks to articles about the related topic. WikiTalk analyses the texts of the Wikipedia articles that it reads, and extracts the hyperlinks that are included in the texts.

In order to switch to a new topic that is related to the current topic, the user just says the name of the NewInfo that is interesting. For example, if the system is talking about Shakespeare and says "Shakespeare was born in Stratford-upon-Avon", the user can say "Stratford-upon-Avon?" and the system will smoothly switch topics and start talking about Stratford-upon-Avon. It does this by going to the NewTopic state (Section 3.3) with Stratford-upon-Avon as the new Topic. This important state transition, from the ContinueTopic state to the NewTopic state, is shown in Figure 3. It is WikiTalk's smooth mechanism for handling smooth topic shifts.

These smooth topic shifts can only be performed when the relevant NewInfo is marked-up with a hyperlink in the Wikipedia text. This is not normally a problem, because the authors of the Wikipedia texts typically provide suitable links, and if the authors don't provide them the links are usually added later by readers and editors. This is one of the reasons why Wikipedia is so convenient and so widely-used.

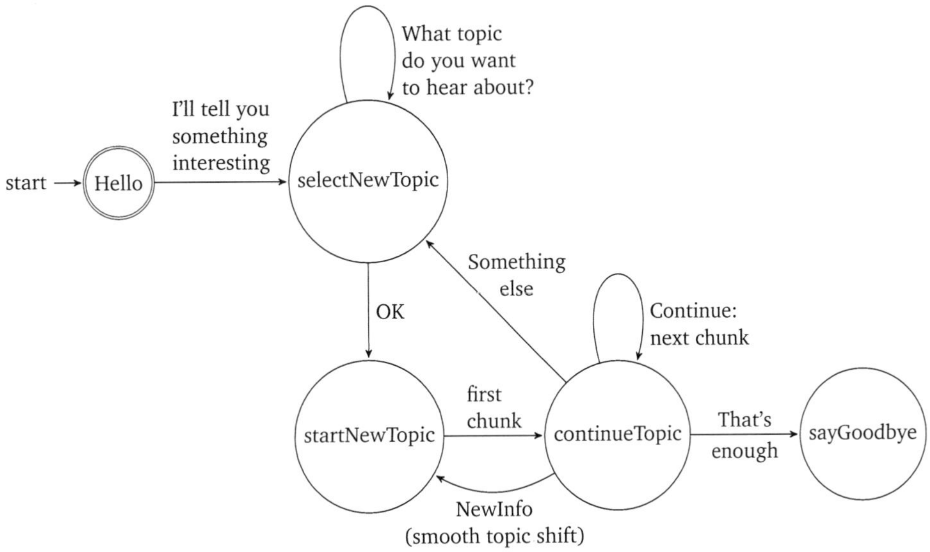

Figure 3: Adding smooth topic shifts.

These hyperlinks were inserted into the texts by the human authors precisely because they represent cognitive links between the concepts in the current text and other concepts in other texts. These hyperlinked NewInfos are precisely the related topics that the user is most likely to want to know more about next. In a normal web browser the user clicks on one of these links in order to pursue a particular concept or topic that may be of greater interest than the topic of the current article. In Wikitalk, the user says one of the link words for the same reason, to move to a new topic in order to pursue a particular concept that may be of greater interest.

4.3 Hyperlinks in Wikipedia

WikiTalk is able to take advantage of the presence of these carefully-chosen links in the Wikipedia articles. However, there are two possible problems that can arise.

The first problem occurs when hyperlinks are added to the first occurrence of a word in an article, but are not added to every subsequent occurrence of the same word in the rest of the article. This problem can be solved by extending the list of words to be recognized, to include all the previously hyperlinked words in the article, not only the hyperlinked words in the latest spoken chunk.

The second problem is that the number of topics in Wikipedia is constantly growing, and therefore more and more topic links are available for linking to more and more words in the articles. The fear is that eventually every word will be hyperlinked. So far this has not happened. However, if every word were hyperlinked, the speech recognizer in WikiTalk would in effect be trying to do open vocabulary speech recognition.

4.4 Changing-Vocabulary Speech Recognition

For effective speech recognition, it is very important to limit the vocabulary to be recognised as much as possible. Open vocabulary speech recognition is currently not feasible as there are simply too many possible words (maybe 300,000 different words in English). An attempt to develop an open-vocabulary speech interface to the Google search engine is described by Franz and Milch (2002).

In WikiTalk, the speech recognizer listens for a relatively small number of the extracted link words, as well as a small number of commands. The commands allow the user to control the system behaviour in order to start, continue, go back, repeat, stop and so on. The list of commands is relatively small and relatively fixed. The list of extracted link words is constantly changing, and its length varies depending on the number of links in each article, but it is nevertheless relatively small. This type of changing-vocabulary speech recognition is naturally far more effective than open-vocabulary recognition.

4.5 Speech Recognition Confidence Scores

WikiTalk uses any speech recognizer that is available, for example Windows Speech Engine or the Aldebaran Nao robot speech components. The details therefore depend on the specific environment, but word spotting is used where possible so that link words can be recognized when they form part of longer phrases such as “Tell me about X”.

Speech recognition confidence scores are used where possible, to decide how to proceed. If a word or phrase is recognized with very high confidence, the system goes ahead immediately without checking. If one word or phrase X is recognized with a significantly higher confidence score than alternatives, but not a very high score, the system asks “Did you mean X?”. If two words X and Y have relatively high scores, the system first asks “Did you mean X?”, and if that is wrong, “Did you mean Y?” If no words or phrases have a high score, the system immediately asks the user to repeat the input.

4.6 Awkward Topic Shifts

The easiest way to select a topic of interest is to navigate to it via the NewInfo links in other topics. However, the user may wish to talk about an entirely new and unrelated topic. This is an awkward topic shift, which needs to be explicitly signalled in human-human dialogues. In WikiTalk, a completely new and unrelated topic can be specified by spelling the first few letters. To help the speech recognizer, this is done with the standard phonetic names for the letters (Alpha, Bravo, Charlie, etc.).

Wikipedia helps this method for spelling a new topic by providing searches for topics starting with any initial sequence of letters, so it is not necessary to spell the whole topic name. After the user gives the first few letters, the system gets a list from Wikipedia of topics that start with those letters. For example, after spelling "Sierra, Hotel, Alpha, Kilo", the system asks the user to select from a list including Shakespeare, Shakira, Shakespeare in Love, Shakers, etc. The system then moves to the NewTopic state (Section 3.3) with the selected topic as the new Topic.

4.7 Suggesting Topics by the System

One of the advantages of using Wikipedia is that the system can easily suggest a topic if the user has no particular topic in mind. One way to do this is based on the "Did you know?" section on the Main Page of the English Wikipedia. This is a short list of new or recently revised articles that is changed every day.

The system selects one of the topics from this list at random and asks the user "Did you know ...?". If the user is interested, this becomes the new topic. If not, another topic is selected from the list and the user is asked again "Did you know ...?" with another topic.

There are many other possibilities for suggesting topics using Wikipedia. For example, there is the "On this day..." section on the Main Page of the English Wikipedia. Topics can be selected at random, or the user's previous interests can be taken into account.

5 An Example Conversation with a Robot

An example dialogue about Shakespeare, using WikiTalk with a robot simulator, is given by Jokinen and Wilcock (2012a). We now give a concrete example of a conversational dialogue with an Aldebaran Nao robot, from a video recording of a user testing session at the 8th International Summer Workshop on Multimodal Interfaces, Metz, 2012.

The robot starts by standing up and telling the user that its favourite topics include Shakespeare, Metz, and Paul Verlaine. The human asks the robot to talk about Metz.

> ROBOT: *Metz is a city in the northeast of France located at the confluence of the Moselle and the Seille rivers. Metz is the capital and the prefecture of both the Lorraine region and the Moselle department. Located near the tripoint along the junction of France, Germany, and Luxembourg, Metz forms a central place of the European Greater Region and the SaarLorLux euroregion.*

Figure 4: Starting the first topic: Metz.

In Figure 4, the robot has downloaded the Wikipedia article about Metz and reads the first paragraph. NewInfo links are extracted for *France, Germany, Luxembourg, Moselle (river), Seille, prefecture, Lorraine (region), Moselle, department, tripoint, Greater Region, SaarLorLux, Euroregion*. They are added to the list of specific items that the speech recognizer will listen for and be specifically ready to recognize. However, the user does not pick out any of these NewInfos, but asks the robot to continue with the Metz topic.

> USER: *Continue.*
>
> ROBOT: *A Celtic oppidum, an important Gallo-Roman city, the Merovingian capital of the Austrasia kingdom, the birthplace of the Carolingian dynasty, a cradle of the Gregorian chant, and one of the oldest republics of the common era in Europe, Metz has a rich 3,000-year-history. The city has been steeped in Romance culture, but has been strongly influenced by Germanic culture due to its location and history.*

Figure 5: Continuing the first topic: Metz.

In Figure 5, the robot continues talking about Metz by reading the second paragraph. In this paragraph the NewInfos are *Celts, oppidum, Gallo-Roman, Merovingian, Austrasia, Carolingian dynasty, Gregorian chant, Common era, Romance languages, Culture of Germany*. They are added to the list of specific items that the speech recognizer will listen for and be specifically ready to recognize.

The user asks about "Celtic", as shown in Figure 6. This is recognized as one of the NewInfos, because the system has extracted the hyperlink to the topic *Celts* that is associated with the word "Celtic".

> USER: *Celtic?*
>
> ROBOT: *The Celts or Kelts were an ethno-linguistic group of tribal societies in Iron Age and Medieval Europe who spoke Celtic languages and had a similar culture.*

Figure 6: Starting the second topic: Celts.

As the user is interested in "Celtic", the robot does not continue reading the main article about Metz, but instead downloads a new Wikipedia article about Celts. It is a natural continuation in the dialogue that the user will select the next topic from the NewInfos, since the human is engaged in the dialogue.

The robot starts reading the first chunk about Celts as shown in Figure 6. The NewInfos here are *Ethnolinguistics, Tribe, Iron Age, Middle Ages, Europe, Celtic languages*. The user asks the robot to talk about Celtic languages. The robot therefore downloads a new Wikipedia article about Celtic languages, and starts reading the first paragraph as shown in Figure 7.

> USER: *Celtic languages?*
>
> ROBOT: *The Celtic or Keltic languages are descended from Proto-Celtic, or "Common Celtic"; a branch of the greater Indo-European language family. The term "Celtic" was first used to describe this language group by Edward Lhuyd in 1707.*

Figure 7: Starting the third topic: Celtic languages.

The NewInfos here are *Proto-Celtic, Indo-European languages, Language Family, Edward Lhuyd*. The user asks about Indo-European languages, and the robot downloads a new Wikipedia article about Indo-European languages, and starts reading the first paragraph as shown in Figure 8.

> USER: *Indo-European?*
>
> ROBOT: *The Indo-European languages are a family of several hundred related languages and dialects. It has about 449 languages and dialects, according to the 2005 Ethnologue estimate, about half belonging to the Indo-Aryan subbranch. It includes most major current languages of Europe, the Iranian plateau, and South Asia, and was also predominant in ancient Anatolia. With written attestations appearing since the Bronze Age, in the form of the Anatolian languages and Mycenaean Greek, the Indo-European family is significant to the field of historical linguistics as possessing the longest recorded history after the Afroasiatic family.*
>
> USER: *Thank you.*
>
> ROBOT: *Thank you. Goodbye.*

Figure 8: Starting the fourth topic: Indo-European languages.

Now the user has heard enough and wants to stop. Saying "Stop" would stop the robot talking about Indo-European languages, but the robot would ask what other topic it should talk about.

Saying "Thank you" tells the robot that the user does not want to hear anything else. The robot replies "Thank you. Goodbye." and sits down.

Note that the words or phrases in the text are not necessarily identical to the names of the linked topics. WikiTalk passes to the speech recognizer the words or phrases that are actually used in the text, because those are the words that the user hears. The system maintains a mapping between these spoken words or phrases and the linked topics. For example, in Figure 6 the spoken word is "Celtic" and the linked topic is *Celts*).

6 Related work

The most famous open-domain dialogue system is still ELIZA (Weizenbaum, 1966). Of course, the reason that ELIZA was capable of maintaining an on-going dialogue about any topic that the user cared to mentioned, without restriction, was that ELIZA did not use any domain knowledge about anything. Since ELIZA, most spoken dialogue systems have been closed-domain systems.

Voice interfaces for search engines have been developed. A speech interface to Google is described by Franz and Milch (2002). The big problem here is speech recognition, as the query is extremely short (median two words), and the vocabulary is large (over 100,000 words). This problem occurs in WikiTalk only when starting a totally new topic unrelated to previous topics. In that case, WikiTalk invites the user to spell the topic. During the conversation, topic shifts to related topics can be handled smoothly because WikiTalk extracts a small list of likely topics based on the NewInfo links. The speech recognizer only needs to recognize a vocabulary of 10 or 20 phrases (including the latest NewInfos and the system commands).

More recently, open-domain question-answering (QA) systems have appeared (Greenwood, 2008). These QA systems use question classifiers, search engines, ontologies, and answer extraction techniques. However, the basic aim of a QA system is to give the correct answer to a specific question, for example, "Q: What is the capital of Lorraine? A: Metz." QA systems are not normally intended to be conversational companions.

A Wikipedia-based question-answering system is described by Buscaldi and Rosso (2006). This QA system has a question type taxonomy and uses Wikipedia "category" entries (for example Category:Fruit) as a kind of ontology. The main aim is to use Wikipedia for validation of the answers, not as a source of topics for conversation.

The Ritel system (Rosset et al., 2006) combines an open-domain question-answering system with a spoken dialogue system. This allows the QA system to be more interactive, to ask clarification questions about the user's question. Kirschner (2007) describes different approaches to Interactive Question Answering. Follow-up questions in interactive QA systems are explored by Kirschner and Bernardi (2009).

These recent more interactive developments bring QA systems closer to dialogue systems. Nevertheless, the aim is still to find the answer to the question, not to talk about a topic. So far, QA systems do not suggest what would be an interesting question to ask.

7 Multimodal capabilities

Following previous work with a robot simulator (Jokinen and Wilcock, 2012a), we have implemented WikiTalk on the Aldebaran NAO robot (Jokinen and Wilcock, 2012b; Csapo et al., 2012). Using a real robot instead of a simulator has enabled us to include multimodal communication features for the robot, especially face-tracking and gesturing. These have been integrated with the spoken conversation system. The robot needs to know whether the human is interested or not in the topic, and the human's proximity and gaze are important for this. Face-tracking is used to provide gaze information which is integrated in the interaction management. The robot also combines suitable nodding, gestures and body language with its own speech turns during the conversation.

For example, beat gestures are small hand movements that do not change the content of the accompanying speech but rather serve a pragmatic function, and emphasise and give rhythm to the speech. Beat gestures usually occur with NewInfos, serving a similar role as intonation to distinguish new and not expected information from the old and expected Topic information. In this way the communication is managed multimodally, and the visual management by gestures emphasises the least known elements to the partner so that the partner surely will notice and understand the new information.

To ensure maximal impact, the agents must make NewInfos as clearly available for the partner as possible, by using suitable lexical items, prosody (pitch, stress, volume, speed), and non-verbal means (gestures, gazing, face expressions), while the partner must be aware of these means in order to integrate the intended meaning in the shared context. Important topics in interaction management are thus related to information presentation: planning and generation of appropriate responses, giving feedback, and managing topic shifts.

An important factor in developing systems that can talk about interesting topics is assessing the level of interest of the user. There are two sides to this: first, how to detect whether the human conversational partner is interested in the topic or not, and second, what should the system do based on this feedback. The approaches to detecting the level of interest are part of the system's external interface, and the decisions about what to do based on this feedback are part of the system's internal management strategy. The external interface must clearly not be limited to purely verbal feedback, but must include intonation, eye-gaze, gestures, body language and other factors in order to assess the interest level correctly. The internal strategy for reacting appropriately to this feedback must decide what to do if the user is clearly interested, or is clearly not interested, and how to continue when the user's interest level is unclear.

Information about the evaluation of the Nao robot system based on the recorded user testing sessions at the 8th International Summer Workshop on Multimodal Interfaces, Metz, 2012 is given in (Csapo et al., 2012) and (Anastasiou et al., 2013).

Acknowledgments

The author is profoundly indebted to Kristiina Jokinen, whose work on the role of NewInfos has been an inspiration for two decades. Many thanks to Dimitra Anastasiou, Adam Csapo, Emer Gilmartin, Jonathan Grizou, JingGuang Han, and Raveesh Meena for implementing and evaluating WikiTalk and the multimodal interaction capabilities on the Nao robot at the 8th International Summer Workshop on Multimodal Interfaces, Metz, 2012.

References

Anastasiou, D., Jokinen, K., and Wilcock, G. (2013). Evaluation of WikiTalk - user studies of human-robot interaction. Proceedings of 15th International Conference on Human-Computer Interaction (HCII 2013).

Buscaldi, D. and Rosso, P. (2006). Mining knowledge from Wikipedia for the question answering task. In *Proceedings of 5th Language Resources and Evaluation Conference (LREC 2006)*, Genoa.

Csapo, A., Gilmartin, E., Grizou, J., Han, J., Meena, R., Anastasiou, D., Jokinen, K., and Wilcock, G. (2012). Multimodal conversational interaction with a humanoid robot. In *Proceedings of 3rd IEEE International Conference on Cognitive Infocommunications (CogInfoCom 2012)*, Kosice.

Franz, A. and Milch, B. (2002). Searching the web by voice. In *Proceedings of 19th International Conference on Computational Linguistics (COLING 2002)*, pages 1213–1217, Taipei.

Greenwood, M., editor (2008). *2nd Information Retrieval for Question Answering Workshop (IR4QA'08)*, Manchester. Workshop at COLING 2008.

Jokinen, K. (2009). *Constructive Dialogue Modelling: Speech Interaction and Rational Agents*. John Wiley & Sons.

Jokinen, K., Tanaka, H., and Yokoo, A. (1998). Context management with topics for spoken dialogue systems. In *Proceedings of Joint International Conference of Computational Linguistics and the Association for Computational Linguistics (COLING-ACL'98)*, pages 631–637, Montreal, Canada.

Jokinen, K. and Wilcock, G. (2011). Emergent verbal behaviour in human-robot interaction. In *Proceedings of 2nd International Conference on Cognitive Infocommunications (CogInfoCom 2011)*, Budapest.

Jokinen, K. and Wilcock, G. (2012a). Constructive interaction for talking about interesting topics. In *Proceedings of Eighth International Conference on Language Resources and Evaluation (LREC 2010)*, Istanbul.

Jokinen, K. and Wilcock, G. (2012b). Multimodal open-domain conversations with the Nao robot. In *Fourth International Workshop on Spoken Dialogue Systems (IWSDS 2012)*, Paris.

Kirschner, M. (2007). Applying a focus tree model of dialogue context to interactive question answering. In *Proceedings of ESSLLI'07 Student Session*, Dublin, Ireland.

Kirschner, M. and Bernardi, R. (2009). Exploring topic continuation follow-up questions using machine learning. In *Proceedings of NAACL HLT 2009: Student Research Workshop*, Boulder, Colorado.

McCoy, K. F. and Cheng, J. (1991). Focus of attention: Constraining what can be said next. In C.L. Paris, W. S. and Mann, W., editors, *Natural Language Generation in Artificial Intelligence and Computational Linguistics)*, pages 103–124. Kluwer Academic Publishers.

Rosset, S., Galibert, O., Illouz, G., and Max, A. (2006). Integrating spoken dialogue and question answering: The RITEL project. In *Proceedings of InterSpeech '06*, Pittsburgh.

Weizenbaum, J. (1966). Eliza - a computer program for the study of natural language communication between man and machine. *Communications of the ACM*, 9(1):36–45.

Author Index